Don't Just Dream It, Do It!

Taking The Leap Into Self-Employment as a Midlife Professional Woman in Less Than 12 Months

Maree Cutler-Naroba

First published by Ultimate World Publishing 2023
Copyright © 2023 Maree Cutler-Naroba

ISBN

Paperback: 978-1-923123-31-1
Ebook: 978-1-923123-32-8

Maree Cutler-Naroba has asserted her rights under the Copyright, Designs and Patents Act 1988 to be identified as the author of this work. The information in this book is based on the author's experiences and opinions. The publisher specifically disclaims responsibility for any adverse consequences which may result from use of the information contained herein. Permission to use information has been sought by the author. Any breaches will be rectified in further editions of the book.

All rights reserved. No part of this publication may be reproduced, stored in or introduced into a retrieval system, or transmitted in any form, or by any means (electronic, mechanical, photocopying, recording or otherwise) without the prior written permission of the author. Any person who does any unauthorised act in relation to this publication may be liable to criminal prosecution and civil claims for damages. Enquiries should be made through the publisher.

Cover design: Ultimate World Publishing
Layout and typesetting: Ultimate World Publishing
Editor: Carmela Julian Valencia

Ultimate World Publishing
Diamond Creek,
Victoria Australia 3089
www.writeabook.com.au

Contents

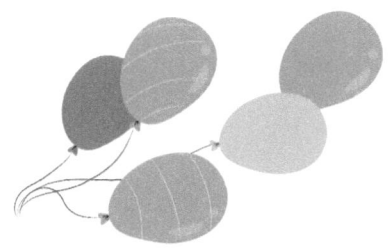

1. Make every twist and turn count	1
2. Shape your business identity	15
3. Smash the mindset gremlins	29
4. Craft your pricing strategy	41
5. Profit with purpose	55
6. Turn your services into products	67
7. Position yourself as a thought leader	81
8. Create footprints online and offline	97
9. Multiply your income streams	111
10. Design a signature system	125
11. Build momentum in your business	139
12. Sustain yourself for the long term	155
Appendix. 5+U Pillars of Business Start-up and Development Model©	169
Other books by Maree Cutler-Naroba	175
About the author	177

1.

Make every twist and turn count

WHAT

As a young girl I had the advantage of a great education. I was always encouraged to read, write, learn, solve mathematical problems and excel in the school environment. I am grateful to my parents for giving me this immense love for learning. However, one thing lacking in my childhood was emotional love and connection – for many years I felt unloved and unwanted and that I was some type of nuisance who needed to stay silent because my opinions or ideas did not matter or were not going to be of good to anyone.

Don´t Just Dream It, Do It!

I was reserved and timid, always too afraid to try something new or make new friends. I wasn't overly confident, and I didn't know how to interact well with groups of people. We were never allowed to play with or have friends around or go to school camps and excursions and we rarely had family members visit us. Growing up as a young woman was not easy – I always felt marginalised and at a disadvantage. I constantly felt like I was on the outside looking in; a bird trapped inside a cage, longing to get out and fly.

As a teenager, I spiralled into an emotional rollercoaster of anorexia, depression and suicide attempts. Friends later encouraged me with their faith journey, and I started to find that personal faith path for myself. This strengthened me and helped me to make healthier choices in my life. My experiences shaped me into a woman with a strong desire to be a spokeswoman for others in situations of injustice – to speak up for girls and women who do not have a voice.

My love for education led me to a teaching career and then into law and entrepreneurship. Teaching empowered me to find my voice, being a lawyer empowered me to speak about situations of injustice and being a businesswoman enabled me to put on those wings and finally fly free (like a butterfly, one of my favourite creatures). I'm out of the cage and into the fullness and joy of what life has to offer.

All of us face twists and turns as we navigate life; it is the rhythm of life. There is no such thing as a perfect life, yet so many of us spend time chasing it. The perfect life may look different for each of us. For some, it might be a digital nomad lifestyle across different countries; for another, it might be founding a charity for a cause they are passionate about; for another, it could be building the home of their dreams in a beautiful, quiet country area. There is nothing wrong with having dreams, goals and aspirations. I love nothing more than sitting with people and hearing their dreams, then brainstorming together on how to activate those dreams.

We need to be intentional about our lives and not just let the days pass by and merge one into another. We need to find our purpose in life, what we are called to do in this world. But we also need to be strongly aware of the twists and turns that can happen; just as the seasons change, so does our life go through different seasons. Challenging seasons are hard, let's just put it out there! They are darn hard to navigate through, and for some of us, those seasons sure do last a very long time.

How we navigate the seasons of life is a true testament to who we are deep in our core. Do we slip into learned helplessness or victim mentality when adversity strikes? Do we fall down the rabbit hole as it were and think, "Oh well, this is my lot in life"? Doing these things is okay for a while because life does hurt so much sometimes. However, don't stay in that place. Be determined to take the twists and turns of your life and use them in some way. One way you can do this, which I have done in my own life, is to take those twists and turns as fuel for self-employment opportunities; in other words, turn your adversities into service through the vehicle of a business.

WHY

Turning adversity into service means using the challenges and difficulties that happened in your life to create a business, an initiative or a project that can help others. It involves finding purpose and meaning in your struggles and using them to positively impact the world so that your legacy is not one of pain and despair but of hope and recovery for the days ahead. The struggles become the why behind what you are doing.

For example, one of my business ventures is centred on dream nurturing. At Dream Nurturer HQ, we work with women recovering from trauma as part of their life journey. Through our tools and coaching, I help women shape their adversity into service so that they can give wings to their magnificent dreams. I use a trauma-informed approach in the coaching sessions, seeking to first hear the story – the narrative of the journey so far. Through inspiration, motivation, tools, tips and brainstorming ideas, we co-design how they can then shape their challenges, struggles and trauma and lean further into a pathway of recovery – whether that's through creating a social enterprise, an impact business, a writing medium or forging a new career pathway.

HOW

Life is not always easy, and many of us have experienced challenges and adversity that have tested our resilience and strength. However, these difficult experiences can also be a catalyst for growth and transformation. In fact, many successful businesses have been built by individuals who have used their personal challenges as inspiration to create products and services that can help others going through similar struggles.

By using your difficult personal experiences as a launching pad, you can inspire others who may be struggling with similar challenges. In essence, making every twist and turn count is about taking what may have been a negative experience and turning it into a positive force for change, both for yourself and others. If you have experienced adversity in your life, there are several steps you can take to turn your experiences into a business that can serve others.

1. Identify your personal story and message

One of my business ventures, as mentioned earlier, is Dream Nurturer HQ, and my tagline for this business is "Giving wings to magnificent dreams".

A butterfly holds significant meaning for me because they fly freely. As you know, a butterfly is first formed in a chrysalis and goes through a metamorphosis to turn from a caterpillar to a butterfly. Life's hard seasons cause us to go into our cocoons. As I've experienced in my own life, we want to shelter ourselves from other adversity, literally and figuratively. We want to curl up in a ball and shut the world out for a while. Isn't that such a picture of what the caterpillar is doing inside the chrysalis?

But we also know that while inside, it undergoes growth and change and strength-building to bust out of the chrysalis. So, too, this happens with us. We may not feel it at the time, but a profound depth and strength build in our dark seasons. When we push through and break out of the chrysalis, our wings represent such beauty and grace that would not be possible had we not spent time inside those "chrysalis" moments we find ourselves in life.

One of the first steps in turning your adversity into service, through the vehicle of business, is to identify your personal story and message. Think about the challenges you have faced and how you overcame them. What lessons have you learned along the way? What unique insights do you have to offer? By identifying your personal story and message, you can begin to create a brand that is authentic and relatable to your target audience. What is it from your life's twists and turns that can become the why behind your business?

Let me provide you with another example. When I was a teenager, I developed anorexia. What a horrible time of my life that was for me and those around me. I truly believed that I was fat and oh-so-ugly when looking in the mirror and that the only way I could remedy this was by getting skinny. I was not a big girl to start with, but my mind raced with unproductive and unhealthy thoughts when it came to my size and looks. Teenage bullying and peer pressure added to the toxic mix. I lived on chewing gum day after day, and even water seemed such an effort to drink.

It was a journey I struggled with until my early 20s. Gradually, I recovered by seeking counselling support, medical assistance and a network of supportive friends. I also turned my adversity and struggles into a pathway to a teaching career wherein I could support and champion young people in pursuit of their dreams. My teaching years were such a privilege when I look back, and I loved nothing more than seeing a young person excel and grow in their confidence, whether that be in the classroom or on the sports field.

I am glad my anorexia days are behind me. Sometimes I look back at them with tremendous regret and beat myself up, thinking what an idiot I was to believe I was a fat chick who needed to be skinny. Once you start treating your body like I did, your body never fully recovers to its optimum level of health.

Health issues have resulted from that time, but I have come to peace with that and have chosen not to let myself go down that rabbit hole of hopelessness and despair.

2. Find your niche

When you have identified your personal story and message, the next step is to find your niche. Who do you want your story to resonate with? Who do you want to reach, impact and encourage with your journey, to pour hope into another? What specific problem or need can you address based on your own experiences? This could be anything from mental health to financial management to physical fitness.

When creating a business, a pivotal point is identifying a niche, and to do this effectively, your business should be a response to a specific need or problem. The solution to that problem can come from your learning experiences of the adversity you have gone through.

My superpower is that of an ideas person. In simpler words, I love taking what seems like nothing and making it into something. I remember once teaching a vocational college class on getting started in business. My friend borrowed my car, which had my teaching box in it. She got held up and did not return the car in time for me to start the lesson. On the desk in the classroom was a ream of paper. I quickly came up with an idea! I gave each student a piece of paper, and their task was to create the best dart they could. We then road-tested the darts to see how far they could fly and then redid the exercise in pairs and small groups. This 30-minute activity became the foundation of the two-hour lesson. I centred on the principle of "What is in your hand?" – what can you do with what is in your hand to create a business?

For instance, the learning I can take away from my time of anorexia is that women are simply beautiful no matter what colour, creed, shape or size – tall or fat or short or skinny or wide. Further, I am in a continual state of learning how to be kinder to myself, something we all need to remind ourselves of as women. My twists and turns led me to have a particular affinity for women in marginalised and disadvantaged situations who do not necessarily have access to ample resources or support to start a business. As a result, my business, SWIRL, empowers and champions women to use what is in their hands to generate self-employment opportunities. In other words, start with the paper dart, as it were, that single bit of paper – the experiences and expertise you have. What can you do with it? Now go do it!

3. Conduct market research

Before you launch your business, it is important to conduct market research to ensure that there is a demand for your product or service. This can involve surveying potential clients, researching your competition and analysing market trends. It can also be helpful to offer some pro bono services or products at reduced prices in this phase to see what appeals to your clients. This phase can also help you refine how you can position yourself in the market and use aspects of your learning experiences to resolve the specific need or problem, which you have identified has a gap in the market. What could you do differently as your entrance point into the market?

When I started SWIRL, I thought of offering coaching packages to help midlife professional women (MLPWs) turn their experiences and expertise into a sustainable business. When I reflected on my SWIRL journey, one thing that stood out to me was that as an MLPW, we do not have many years to get into business; if it is a decision we have made to do, then let's just get on with it!

In speaking with other MLPWs considering taking the leap into self-employment, this is one of the common points that came up: "If I am going to do it, then I want to do it now!" From this, I decided to develop a coaching service that particularly enables MLPWs to quickly transition from employment to self-employment within a 12-month period. By deeply understanding your target audience and the competitive landscape, you can develop a business strategy that is effective and sustainable.

4. The launching pad

Starting a business that helps others by fulfilling a need in the marketplace can be a way to generate income and be a vehicle for fuelling your passion and purpose in life. Clients will be attracted to your authenticity and wisdom because you walk your talk – they will see that you provide strength and understanding through the solutions and services you offer. Expertise and skill are needed in running a business, but I tell you, genuine passion and drive for your business, the business niche you specialise in, are what will speak louder than anything else.

Once you have identified your niche and conducted market research, the next step is to create a business plan. This should include a vision and mission statement, a description of your products and/or services, marketing actions and financial projections. Developing a comprehensive business plan ensures you are prepared to launch and grow your business. Your business plan becomes a roadmap of sustainability. You also need to build a support network to help you along the way. This can include mentors, coaches and other business owners who have experienced similar challenges. By building a support network, you can stay motivated, receive feedback and learn from the experiences of others.

In creating your roadmap, you then get underway with actions such as creating marketing collateral – like a logo, business capability statement and social media pages. Through promoting your business effectively and building a strong brand, you can begin to attract clients and generate revenue.

In the appendix of this book, there is a **5+U Pillars of Business Start-up and Development Model** © that walks you through a series of questions that cover each important pillar of your business: Strategy, Legal Compliance, Marketing, Operations, Finances and You (U), the business owner. In the following chapters you will find tips, hints, examples and tools on how you market and grow your business.

Being in business can be challenging and is not for the faint-hearted. You do need the courage of a lion to overcome some of the barriers you will face in building your business. But remember that you are using your twists and turns of life, turning your adversity into service, and the strength you have is more than you probably will ever realise. Don't give up at the first hurdle! Turning your adversity into service is not easy, but it can be an incredibly rewarding experience. By using your personal experiences to create a business that can serve others, you can find meaning and purpose in your work and make a positive impact on the world.

My story shows a midlife professional woman who has woven her expertise and experiences together to shape service-based business ventures for other such women, positioning herself and growing for impact and legacy.

As I have done, you can too! Don't just dream it, do it!

WHAT IF

If you decide not to turn your adversity into service, allow me to gently let you know that you may miss out on the opportunity to make a positive impact on the world and help others going through similar struggles. You may also miss out on the personal growth and fulfilment that comes from finding purpose and meaning in your hardships. By not using your twists and turns of life to shape your business ventures, you may also miss out on the potential benefits that come with entrepreneurship.

If you choose not to address and process your past struggles, you may carry them with you into other aspects of your life, such as personal relationships or other professional pursuits. This can lead to feelings of stagnation and can impact your physical, emotional and mental health. Recovery is never ever an easy road because life's seasons do leave a mark on us, but those seasons do not have to become an excuse for not taking flight with the magnificent wings we were born with.

Ultimately, not using your experiences to shape the *what* and *how* of your business ventures may mean that your struggles and hardships go untapped as a source of inspiration and motivation. It may also mean that others miss out on the support and guidance you could provide them through your own experiences.

Don´t Just Dream It, Do It!

It is important to remember that turning your adversity into service does not mean you have to be a perfect role model or have everything figured out. It simply means that you are willing to use your experiences to help others and find purpose and fulfilment in the process. You will never know the person you will become as a result of making the choice to turn your adversity into service unless you take those first steps.

3 Action Questions

1. What have been some of your life's twists and turns that have shaped you into the woman you are today?

Hindsight, they say, is 20/20. Looking back on your life experiences can provide you with a clearer perspective, allowing you to see how those experiences have shaped you, identify your strengths, define your purpose and recognise the valuable resources you possess.

Have you been through a health scare? Rebounded from a job loss? Lost a loved one? These experiences may be incredibly challenging in the moment, but in hindsight can reveal aspects of yourself that will propel you in the direction of your purpose and passion.

2. What learning from those twists and turns do you think you can draw on in considering the self-employment opportunities you want to transition into as an MLPW?

Examining your past will give you clarity on the strengths and skills you've developed along the way. For instance, working with a demanding boss may have improved your problem-solving ability or people skills or working in retail or customer-facing roles may have developed your communication skills.

Think of your experiences, drawbacks and wins as lessons that have equipped you with the skills and strengths you need to succeed. Recognising these strengths is essential because it will give you a foundation to build on when venturing into self-employment.

3. What will be the niche for your business, and how will you address the specific need or problem of that niche?

What are you passionate about? Identifying your purpose and passions will be instrumental when making the leap into self-employment. The why behind your desire to pursue self-employment will guide you on what business niche aligns best with your passions, strengths and purpose.

Your unique experiences and perspective are valuable assets that can help you build a compelling personal brand that resonates with your target audience. Let's say you have a background in healthcare and have faced challenges accessing healthcare services in your rural community. You find a shortage of specialised home healthcare services in your region due to its remote nature. Your target audience might be elderly residents in your rural community who require regular medical check-ups and assistance with daily living. In this case, you have identified a niche that serves an existing need in the community and suits your background and personal interests.

2.

Shape your business identity

WHY

You can use self-employment as a vehicle to harness and bring together your experiences and expertise. You are in the driver's seat, and it is your decision as to how you want to drive this vehicle, how often, for what purpose, on what roads and who you want to have with you inside (your staff, clients, stakeholders, etc).

Like you, your business needs an identity that sets it apart and announces its purpose, mission and unique value proposition. A business's identity is like its personality and plays a central role in how clients perceive and interact with that business. Whether you are thinking of your favourite family coffee shop down the street or mega brands like Apple, when you walk into a business, you already have an impression of what to expect, how you will feel and whether you will get value for your money. This is because businesses, just like people, have identities that shape how we think of them.

From this perspective, consider the identity you want your target audience to have for your business. Do you want to be the brand that people think about when they want prompt, reliable services or the brand that people go to when the better option is closed? Do you want to be the business that people take a detour to visit or the business that people drive past to get to a better option? The kind of identity you create for your business will set your venture apart from the competition and communicate who you are, what you stand for and what value you offer.

Think of your business identity as the blueprint that will set the tone for marketing, decision-making and client relationships, contributing significantly to your business's overall success and longevity. A well-defined business identity sets clear expectations for clients. For instance, when you walk into your favourite restaurant, you arrive with certain expectations regarding service quality and the calibre of cuisine. These expectations are bedded in the well-defined identity the restaurant has painstakingly crafted over time.

Whether consciously or subconsciously, clients form impressions based on a business's identity, which then influence their emotions, decisions and loyalties. This is why you want to take time to carefully consider how to craft a compelling identity for your business – one that will foster trust and credibility and set you apart from the rest.

Shaping a strong and authentic business identity often involves drawing from your personal experiences, identifying pain points and leveraging your unique strengths. Consider the gap your business can fill – one that existing businesses may not be addressing adequately. What solution can your business offer to resolve a pressing problem for your target audience?

The authenticity of your brand purpose and vision lies at the core of a compelling business identity. When your brand purpose is founded in a genuine desire to make a positive impact or provide a meaningful solution, it not only builds trust but also inspires loyalty among your clients.

For instance, if you've experienced the frustration of struggling to find eco-friendly household products in your local area and you are passionate about sustainability, you might start a business that specialises in providing eco-conscious alternatives. Your personal connection to the issue and commitment to offering a solution that aligns with your values will resonate with like-minded clients seeking similar products. This authenticity in your brand's purpose and vision can set the tone for your entire business identity and significantly contribute to its success.

A business identity that has a compelling story is more engaging. When your brand identity includes a narrative that reflects your journey, purpose and values, it becomes a powerful tool for storytelling, deepening the connection with your audience. People remember stories much more effectively than raw data or facts. When your business has a compelling narrative at its core, it's more likely to stick into clients' minds so they can recall the business when they need your products or services.

Ultimately, a strong business identity goes beyond visual elements and branding; it encompasses your core values, mission and how you engage with your audience. When done right, it becomes the heart and soul of your venture, helping you not only survive but thrive in a competitive landscape.

WHAT

When it comes to business, one size does **not** have to fit all. Every business is unique, and its identity is shaped by a combination of factors, including the *what*, *why*, *who* and *how*. Let's break down how these elements help in shaping a distinctive business identity:

What you do (Products or Services):

Your products or services are a fundamental part of your business identity. They define the value you provide to clients and the problems you solve for them. What you do sets the stage for your brand and market positioning.

Why you exist (Purpose and Mission):

Your business's purpose and mission statement answer why you exist beyond making a profit. They communicate the positive impact you aim to make in the world and help you connect with clients who share your values.

Whom you serve (Target Market):

Identifying your target market is crucial for an authentic business identity. It's about understanding your ideal clients' demographics, behaviours and pain points.

Unique value proposition (UVP):

What is the unique combination of benefits and solutions that you offer to your target market? Clearly defining your UVP in your messaging and branding helps clients understand why they should choose your business over others.

How you deliver (Client experience):

The way you deliver your products or services is a key part of your business identity. What kind of client experience do you offer and how do you create value?

HOW

Before you can shape your expertise into an authentic, sustainable business, you need to dig down to your why and what. In other words, you need to go inward before you can go outward. Take a portion of your time to personally reflect on what drives you from your heart – your heart DNA, your values and your inner core. Articulating your *why* will shape your *what* (your vision); your *what* needs to be connected to your *why*. Your what and why will then enable you to shape your *how* (your mission) – how will you use your expertise to fulfil your vision?

It is important to consider your target market and complete an analysis of their primary characteristics. In other words, you need to get inside the head of your ideal client. Your target market needs to be specific – for example, "Women in their 40s who hate exercising" rather than just "Women who want to get fit". Have no more than two or three target markets, otherwise your marketing will end up being a scattergun approach. You cannot be all things to all people, no matter the level of your expertise.

Once you have your business underway, regularly use extensive statistical profiling to identify as much as you can about your target market and keep this profiling updated as the needs of the market can change. Market research could be conducted by a marketing student from one of your local universities; students are always looking for such work to expand their portfolios.

Discover what your target market wants versus what they need. You need to understand what your target market wants and then drill down to what they need. This is because, in marketing, you market to what they want (to emotionally engage the client) and not to what they need. For example, a business wants to incorporate videos on its website to engage more clients and convert each engagement into a sale. What this business needs are engaging, authentic videos and not mere old-style and boring talking-head videos. If you were a Video Marketing Expert, your marketing material would use questions such as, "Do you want more visitors to your website?" and "Do you want more clicks to be turned into sale ticks?" This will engage clients with your expertise in contrast to words such as, "We create videos to help you market your business."

Shape your business identity

As your business develops and grows, continue to identify trends in your area of expertise and within your target market that could assist the direction of your business. For instance, many people in their 40s and older use Facebook, but those in their 20s and 30s have turned away from it and prefer sites such as Instagram and TikTok. Use online trend polls that are based on what your potential clients or market niche are asking about. In what ways can your range of services assist such clients? Listening consistently to your existing and prospective clients is essential – what are they saying, wanting and needing? Be flexible and willing to change!

Always think about your business from your target market's point of view. Your **unique value proposition** (UVP) is one of your most essential messages; two to three sentences are an ideal length for this message. Your UVP needs to be a powerful and succinct statement describing how you are unique and therefore differentiates you and your services from your competitors in the market. There is no one-size-fits-all template for writing a UVP, but a great technique is understanding the pain points of your target market.

Think about when you have been in pain, such as a sprained ankle. You do everything you can to get rid of the pain – ice the ankle, elevate the ankle, strap the ankle when walking, get pain medication and such. What I'm saying is, it is **not** a human need to want to be in pain. In fact, most of us, at even a small level of pain, say, "I will do anything to get out of this pain right now."

Apply that analogy to your target market! What "treatment" (solution) will your business "prescribe" (deliver) to alleviate a client from their pain? You must touch the pain point/s to get a reaction (sale!) from the client. Consider this example:

Pain: The kids are starving, but Mum and Dad are too tired to cook.

UVP: Five nutritious, hearty, in-season family meals delivered to your door every Sunday evening by 7 pm, Monday to Friday. Simply heat and eat within 20 minutes.

Your UVP is the very core of what your service is offering; it needs to be compelling so you can use it across your online and offline marketing materials. More importantly, you need to be able to deliver on your promises. Your UVP can be written in the service itself, your offer or your guarantee. For a make-up artist, this could look like:

Service: A make-up technique that will instantly have you looking glamorous and confident, just like your favourite celebrity.

Offer: You can learn this simple make-up technique that makes you look like your favourite celebrity in just 10 minutes.

Guarantee: If you don't feel glamorous and confident the first time you use this make-up technique and head off to a social occasion, then we will refund your money.

Creating a business name is an exciting part of the start-up phase. Don't rush what you want to call your business, as the name will reflect you in the marketplace. You also need to consider what will be your domain name, tagline, fame name and logo. Note that your business name and domain name do not have to be identical. You need to consider what types of words your prospective client would enter as part of their research when looking for the answer to the problem you are able to resolve for them.

For example, your business name may be Chandy Chiropractor because you want to name the business after your surname (Chandy). But for the URL, you could decide on mybackissosore.com.au, as these may be the words a prospective client would use, especially for those unfamiliar with the term *chiropractor* or unsure what a chiropractor does – that is, being able to help fix sore backs.

Next, create a catchy tagline to showcase on your website and social media platforms. Your tagline should not be more than six to eight words and needs to emotionally engage your prospective client. While your tagline is not the same as your UVP, it will contain the essence of your UVP, the heart centre of your business.

For example, the heart centre of my business, Dream Nurturer HQ, is strengthening and encouraging people to unlock and tap into their dreams and then provide them with ideas on how to act on those dreams. Hence, the tagline I decided on was using the word *idea* as an acronym: "Igniting Dreams, Evoking Action". For a graphic designer, the tagline could say, "We brand your business with impact" or "We bring your business passion to life through branding".

Next, create a fame name. A fame name is a personal headline that grabs the attention of your target market, just like how Supernanny and The Naked Chef do. In my case, my fame name is **Dream Nurturer.**

A fame name is easy to remember; it tells people who you are and where you are in the market. Are you the person we want to learn from, work with or buy from? Continuing the example of a graphic designer, their fame name could be *The Branding Guru, Graphic Design Strategist* or *The Brand-It Specialist*.

Lastly, consider your logo. Your logo needs to be distinctive and impactful, as it's the first thing prospective clients will see when they look at your online and offline marketing materials. Before you approach a logo designer, sketch some ideas for your logo – consider shape, colours and other elements and collect a range of logos you like to gain ideas.

WHAT IF

You probably have a friend you turn to when you're in a tricky situation and need a diplomatic approach and a different friend who is always ready to help in matters of relationships. Each person in your life adds unique value based on who they are and their distinct perspective. In that regard, businesses are no different. A business with a strong identity fosters better connections with its clients by creating an emotional connection. Without a strong business identity, clients may find it challenging to form a meaningful connection with your company, which may lead to:

Lack of clarity: Without a well-defined identity, your business may struggle to convey its purpose and values clearly.

Difficulty building trust: Trust is a crucial factor in client relationships. A weak business identity can make it harder for clients to trust your brand, leading them to competitors they find more trustworthy.

Lower brand recognition: A strong identity can make your brand memorable and recognisable. Without it, it will be difficult for clients to recall or distinguish your brand.

Missed emotional connection: Strong brands create emotional connections with clients. Without a clear identity, your business may struggle to evoke positive emotions and sentiments in your target audience.

Difficulty in niche targeting: Niche markets often require a specialised and unique identity. Without it, your business may find it challenging to cater to the specific needs of a niche target audience.

Limited brand loyalty: Strong identities foster brand loyalty. Without it, clients may lack the emotional attachment that keeps them coming back.

3 ACTION QUESTIONS

1. Are you an MLPW who dislikes the questions: What is your talent? What is your strength? What is your passion?

Does your expertise and experiences make you multi-skilled and multi-passionate? You are even often asked, "Can you not decide what you are doing yet?" I have heard this question many times over, and the beauty of being in business is that you can use who you are to shape what you do.

For instance, I have several business ventures because I am not wired to do just one thing. So, do not be afraid to explore different ventures if you have more than one passion or feel drawn to multiple things.

2. Do you have some ideas about what you want to do in your business, but currently they are either just in your head or a few scribbles in a notebook?

Get a large piece of paper and some texters. Write all the ideas of the products and/or services you envision your business will offer over a timeframe of two to five years.

Once you have done your first layer of six to ten ideas, use a different coloured texter and go back to each idea. Create two to three more ideas off each original one; do this for three to four layers.

3. Now look over all the ideas you have written down. Is there a thread, a theme or a pattern that stands out from the types of products or services you want to offer?

That thread, theme and pattern will give you a good starting point for what will sit at the core of your business. This core, often referred to as your business's DNA or identity, serves as the foundation upon which you can build your brand, make strategic decisions and shape your interactions with clients.

When I did this exercise for starting out my own business, I saw that the core theme was all about wanting to get people from Point A to Point B – whether that was through creating a business plan or creating a career/work plan for them or helping organise the systems for their business. My core passion was education, and it was education that flowed through the service and product ideas I had.

3.

Smash the mindset gremlins

WHY

Is the fear of the unknown stopping you from launching your own business? Do you fear failure, having to return to the corporate workplace, not getting enough money, not getting clients? All these are valid fears that a lot of us, as MLPWs, have.

We are strong, independent women who have pushed through challenging times and difficult seasons. Sometimes we rationalise that the status quo of staying in our current employed roles is easier than trying to start building our own business. Before we even start, we self-sabotage.

Recognise that self-sabotage is a trauma response to the fear of success – the fear that what we do will never be good enough. What is the answer to this fear and other mindset gremlins, like self-doubt and lack of confidence, as well as that loop of thoughts like "What I do does not count" and "No one wants to listen to me"?

The answer is to **smash the mindset gremlins**. There is no gentle way about it. You must get the big metaphorical axe out and chop off the roots of those fears once and for all. As a woman in business, you need to get comfortable with being uncomfortable; get out of your comfort zone.

I recall going on a driving adventure, heading from the urban heights of where I live to meet a girlfriend at a cafe in a country township. I always get myself somewhat stressed when finding new places. Somehow, I think I will get horribly lost and end up in some place completely opposite of where I am to be – as you will note, I am already self-sabotaging before I even turn the key ignition on!

Hubby had given me straightforward instructions, plus the GPS on the mobile was on standby. With a sigh of relief, I got myself to the country township but not quite to the venue. I gave the venue a phone call and was told I was only minutes away; I just needed to make a right turn and then look for a fork in the road where there was a driveway. Finally, I made it and arrived at a beautiful Roman art deco cafe.

Before I left for this new route, I sought some advice – from Hubby, in this instance, since he had been to the township before – and I also put on my GPS. Both things helped me get to the township and then to the venue.

Smash the mindset gremlins

How often do we not get out of our comfort zone because we fear that we will end up on some other road, as it were, or it is too exhausting to even try because the stress and anxiety levels go up? However, if we never allow ourselves permission to get out of our comfort zone or our usual routes of doing life, we will never get to discover new things, meet new people and simply breathe in the fresh air of new experiences.

Comfort zones are often governed by fear – fear of failure, rejection or the unknown. Stepping out of your comfort zone helps you confront and overcome these fears, allowing you to move forward with confidence. Undoubtedly taking a step into the unknown can be scary, and you may have doubts about what will happen or if you have what it takes to run a successful venture. But, on the other side of that fear are the dreams and passions you want to pursue, as well as the greater purpose that can give you a new lease of life. What would it take for you to bet on yourself and take that leap?

It's important to remember that you're not alone. Many now-successful entrepreneurs experienced the same initial apprehension and uncertainty when they ventured into self-employment. They took the leap, learned along the way and found their path to success. Before achieving their goals, many experienced failures – a natural part of entrepreneurship. Instead of fearing it, view it as a stepping stone to success. Embracing challenges and stepping out of your comfort zone is where personal and professional growth happen, and each obstacle is an opportunity to learn and become more resilient.

Self-employment is a continuous learning journey. You'll acquire new skills, gain experience and become more confident over time. Remember that self-employment provides a way for you to shape your own destiny. This independence can be incredibly empowering and, for most entrepreneurs, makes all the growing pains, fears and challenges at the beginning well worth it.

WHAT

My experience in my work with clients and my own life experience is that as women, we struggle to believe in our value and that what we do, who we are and the impact we make on our family, workplaces, businesses and communities does make a difference. We struggle to believe that the ideas and dreams deep within our souls need to be awakened and that we need to paint our world with them. We struggle to believe that we are amazing partners or wives, daughters, mums, community members, business owners and such.

Because we struggle to believe in our value, we do not always fully develop and use our gifts, talents, skills and experiences. It is time we believe in who we are and the impact we do have and can have. As women, we can bring unique perspectives and insights to the table. Your experiences, challenges and successes have shaped your viewpoint, and this perspective is an asset in problem-solving and decision-making.

Impostor syndrome is a common experience, especially among high-achieving women. It is important to recognise that it is driven by fear and self-doubt and not a reflection of one's actual abilities and accomplishments. A fear of failure can be a powerful driver of impostor syndrome. People may believe that if they don't meet their own or others' expectations, they'll be exposed as frauds. Striving for perfection can also make you feel like an impostor and further fuel your self-doubt. It is important to recognise when these feelings of self-doubt arise and challenge them with evidence of your capabilities and achievements. This includes reframing your thoughts, seeking support from mentors or peers and focusing on your accomplishments as evidence of your competence.

HOW

If you are struggling to believe in your value as a potential businesswoman, read, listen to and get involved with inspirational businesswomen – this can be a powerful first step. But to get on with your business ideas and move from feeling inferior to one of value, you must believe in yourself as a business owner. Who or what is currently filling up the seats in your "plane" (business)? Who or what should be part of your business? Who or what is causing turbulence and what can you do about that? What is your business plan – your business goals, what you would like to do, what you want to achieve?

Learning to believe in who you are and what you can achieve as a business owner is not some overnight transformation. It takes time; it takes points of reflection, of change, of transition, of churning in the stomach, of breathing slowly as you get rid of the turbulence in your life. A great way to capture these times of reflection and transition is using a journal or notebook. This helps you see your personal and business progress and the challenges ahead.

Doubt is one of the biggest killers of dreams. We doubt ourselves; we doubt our abilities, and we doubt that we ever really have a dream. We doubt that we can make a difference. We doubt that we have the time, the money and the resources.

Don't Just Dream It, Do It!

Women of value, get rid of doubt in your life right now! Action will overcome doubt. A footstep today will get you closer to your dreams than a footstep you wait to take tomorrow. Doubt breeds negativity and shuts off creativity. Don't let your dreams be submerged in doubt, but let them be submerged in daring to believe you can see your dreams come alive.

As women, so many of us are trapped in fear. Fear is our prison, and it takes guts, determination and a fighting spirit to choose not to let fear keep us locked inside our dreams. Fear has always been a challenge for me. Many, many times I have allowed fear to hold me back, push me down, render me without a voice and dismiss my ideas and goals as useless and of little impact.

I remember a three-day trip Hubby and I did to Queenstown, New Zealand. On our second day, Hubby said he would like to do a bungee jump. My heart began to race (even though it wasn't me who would be doing it!), and I began to think about his fear of heights.

Great, I thought to myself. *Just the perfect solution to overcoming a fear of heights – let's jump off a high platform. Not!*

Hubby went on to explain that when he was at university, he had done a case study on the bungee jumping business in Queenstown. At that time, he had said to himself, "To overcome my fear of heights, I am going to do bungee jumping one day!" (Don't worry, gals, sometimes a man's logic is too complicated!)

So, off I went to the viewing deck as Hubby climbed the platform. My palms were sweating, and I was sure I wouldn't be able to hold the camera straight. I waited and waited. I saw a big line and thought, *Oh, that's good he won't be first.*

Smash the mindset gremlins

I heard the instructors talking about the ropes and pulleys. The next minute (or perhaps it was a little longer), I heard this joyous, booming yell. The lady standing next to me said, "Wow, that was loud!"

I realised it was Hubby, and I completely missed the shot (thank goodness for the commercial photo)! I was frozen at the moment. I then looked up and saw Hubby scaling the platform again! For the next hour, he somehow volunteered himself as chief cheerleader. You could hear him cheering on each person as they came to the platform, telling them they could do it – Just take a step, another step and then let go and fly like a bird!

That day I saw a fear-fighter in action. I saw the sheer joy of when Hubby broke through the fear and began to fly, as it were. In allowing himself to break free, he then started to set others free. What a powerful analogy!

What fears do you need to bust through? What step can you do today and then what step can you do tomorrow and beyond to edge you closer and closer to flying free onto your goals, dreams, passion and purpose?

There are many reasons we can be locked in fear. Growing up in a dysfunctional household, fear and anxiety crippled me well into my early 20s. I had to take hold of the meaning of F.E.A.R – either to Forget Everything And Run or Face Everything And Rise!

I had to start to face some pain and allow myself a journey of healing. In doing so, I recognised that I had a choice to break free. Fear, at times, can still lock me down, and I can feel my stomach churning as the panic attack arises. But I focus on the choice I have, and that choice is that I am a fear-fighter – feeling the fear and doing it anyway, as that well-known quote goes.

As women starting out in business, wow, do the fears start coming at full speed when we decide to step out! I want to tell you this: Your business will impact many, and it will inspire other women to start their own businesses too; it's a ripple effect. You don't have to start out with a platform jump; just start with freelancing some of your skills and some small gigs until you build up your confidence.

WHAT IF

The biggest regret most people have at the end of their lives is the opportunities or chances they failed to take due to fear, lack of self-belief or simple fear of the unknown. Without opening yourself up to new opportunities and experiences, you may very well stay within the safe comfort zone you are used to, but at what cost?

>**Stagnation:** Self-employment often requires adaptability and continuous learning. If you are resistant to change, your business may struggle to evolve and thrive.

>**Limiting beliefs:** A fixed mindset may lead to limiting beliefs about your abilities and potential.

>**Lack of resilience:** Without a resilient mindset, you may struggle to bounce back from failures and even give up on your entrepreneurial aspirations too soon.

Regret: You may look back and wonder, "What if you had taken the leap and embraced the opportunities before you?"

Unfulfilled potential: MLPWs often have a wealth of experience and skills to offer. Failing to change your mindset can result in unfulfilled potential and a missed chance to make a significant impact in your chosen field.

Financial insecurity: Staying in a fixed mindset and resisting self-employment can limit your income potential. Self-employment often offers the possibility of greater financial independence and control.

Lack of passion: Pursuing self-employment without a growth mindset can lead to lack of passion and enthusiasm for your work. Passion is often the driving force behind successful entrepreneurial ventures.

3 ACTION QUESTIONS

1. When you start out on something new, what gets your stress and anxiety levels up?

Are you worried about failure or what others may think of you if you fail? Is your stress due to overthinking and trying to get everything just right from the onset? Are you anxious about your finances or the possibility of failure?

Identifying the cause of your stress and anxiety is key to smashing the mindset gremlins that may impede your progress. Once you are aware of the negative thoughts and beliefs you need to reframe, you will have the power to develop a more positive and growth-oriented mindset.

2. What can you put in place, who could you speak to or what resources could you read or listen to that will help reduce your stress and anxiety levels when starting your business?

Having that self-awareness means you are halfway to smashing the self-doubt and fear gremlins. I am not the best flyer – my stomach starts churning, my palms get sweaty, and I start doing some breathing techniques to calm myself. Reading an engaging magazine and sucking on some mints can also help! Can anyone else relate?

But the biggest battle is in my mind – I need to believe that the plane and the pilot will do their thing, which is getting the plane from A to B. Yes, there might be some turbulence on the way, a few wobbles here and there, but I imagine the plane flying smoothly through the clouds and landing. I can't say I have perfected this art of believing that as the plane goes up, it will come down, and I will be fine; but I work on it because I don't want that fear to stop me from travelling to new places!

3. What would you do if your fear or anxiety were not there? How would you act? What steps would you take, and how would you approach your venture?

Imagining how you would act if fear or anxiety were not present can be a powerful exercise to help you gain clarity and confidence in pursuing your venture. This exercise can help you visualise the empowered and confident version of yourself who is free from fear and anxiety. While it's natural to experience these emotions at times, recognising how you would act in their absence can give you clarity on what you need to do or the approach you need to take.

Taking the time to visualise a different, more empowered reality whenever you find yourself stalling can be an effective technique to overcome your fears and regain momentum in your venture. Visualisation allows you to get out of your head, step out of your current mindset and view your situation from a different angle. This shift in perspective can reveal new insights and solutions to the challenges you're facing.

4.

Craft your pricing strategy

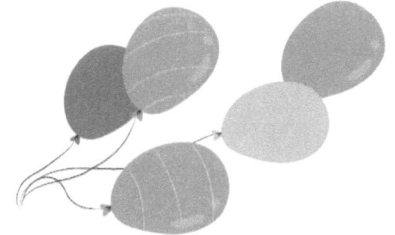

WHY

Are you a midlife professional woman (MLPW) who has runs on the board, including some level of management experience? What price do you put on that? Are you an MLPW with qualifications and training but is keen to upskill or in the process of upskilling, like pursuing an MBA or a counselling or coaching/mentoring qualification? What price do you put on that?

As a newbie to business, one of the most challenging areas you will find is pricing and packaging your goods and services. There is a tendency to either underprice or overprice the **Triple**

E: experiences, education and expertise. Crafting your pricing strategy means gaining a deep understanding and control over how you set, adjust and manage the prices of your products and services to achieve your business goals effectively.

You need to make money in your business! Pricing is part art and part science. It involves finding the balance that works for you among profitability, paying yourself (yes, you can pay yourself!), market demand and client satisfaction. It is important to take time, both at the beginning and throughout your business journey, to consider the pricing of your products and services.

Pricing is not a matter of set and forget. Your pricing strategy positions you in the market. It defines whether you are a luxury brand, a budget-friendly option or in-between. Your positioning influences which client segments you attract. To attract the right client to your business, your pricing should align with your target market's expectations and budget.

Remember that a successful business idea not only meets a need in the market but also understands and caters to the specific circumstances of the target audience. For instance, if you plan to open a business in an area with low purchasing power, consider bundling products or services together to make them more affordable for clients with limited disposable income. The clients will perceive greater value in purchasing a bundle than buying individual items separately. Bundling can also allow you to target different market segments since you can offer basic packages or products at lower prices and premium options with added features or benefits at slightly higher prices.

Craft your pricing strategy

For example, consider Jocelyn, who is starting a landscaping and gardening business. Through market research, she determines that many homeowners in her area look for affordable maintenance plans. She decides to offer tiered pricing packages, including basic maintenance, seasonal landscaping and custom garden design. These packages address her target clients' unique needs and budget constraints, ensuring she can attract clients at different price points. With this approach, she ensures a consistent stream of income throughout the year, making her business financially sustainable.

By conducting thorough market research and understanding the specific needs, pain points and preferences of your niche market, you can design pricing and packaging options that directly address those requirements. A one-size-fits-all approach doesn't consider the nuances of different client segments, so it can result in missed opportunities to attract and engage potential clients who are seeking tailored solutions.

Remember that a good pricing and packaging strategy will help you strike the balance between offering your clients value for their money and remaining profitable. When you overprice your products or services, you risk pricing yourself out of the market. Clients may perceive your offerings as too expensive and seek more affordable alternatives. This can lead to lower sales volume and missed revenue opportunities. On the other hand, if you underprice yourself, you may attract clients yet not be able to cover your costs (including paying yourself), resulting in financial losses. Also, clients tend to question the quality and value of heavily discounted products or services.

It is also important to remember that market dynamics change over time, so your approach to pricing and packaging should be flexible and adaptable. Even if you do not get it right the first time, regularly reviewing and adjusting your pricing based on market dynamics, client feedback and cost changes can help you stay competitive and sustainable in the long term.

For example, Sarah, who runs a small farm-to-table catering service, initially started her business with a focus on serving traditional Australian cuisine and locally sourced ingredients. Sarah had a limited menu, showcasing classic Australian dishes. However, she noticed a growing interest in health-conscious catering among her clients. To cater to the health-conscious, Sarah introduced more plant-based and vegetarian dishes, as well as gluten-free and vegan options. This shift in menu offerings resulted in higher prices but appealed to a broader client base, which meant more clients and, thus, more revenue.

When coming up with a pricing and packaging strategy, always leave some room to adjust to changing client preferences, as these can change rapidly due to shifts in lifestyle, culture or emerging trends. By maintaining flexibility, you can adjust your offerings to align with new client preferences.

WHAT

As a new business owner embarking on your entrepreneurial journey, the excitement of bringing your product or service to the market is palpable (along with a few nerves!). Your vision, dedication and passion are the driving forces behind your venture, and you may already have a clear idea of the value your product or service holds. However, it's crucial to recognise that businesses exist within a dynamic ecosystem, where you need to strike a balance between the perceived value of your product or service, client expectations and prevailing market conditions.

When pricing and packaging your products and services, the three key elements to factor are your client expectations, competitor analysis and market trends. The perceived value of your product or service should harmonise with the expectations of your target clients. It's not solely about how much you believe your offering is worth but also how much value your clients perceive in it. Often, there is a gap between the two, and you have to be realistic and honest with yourself about this. What problems does your product solve for them? Are your competitors offering a similar product? Are they providing similar products and services at a lower cost, or do they command a premium for unique features? Understanding your place in the competitive landscape will enable you to set a pricing strategy that effectively differentiates your product or service while remaining competitive.

HOW

The foundational step in crafting an effective pricing and packaging strategy for your business involves comprehensively understanding the costs of producing, delivering and marketing your products and services. This means that before you can craft a pricing and packaging strategy, you first need to conduct a cost analysis of the expenses associated with producing, delivering and marketing your products or services. This includes direct costs (materials and labour) and indirect costs (rent, utilities and marketing expenses), as well as your salary – what you want to earn as an MLPW. So often this last cost is not one that business owners put in their cost analysis. Why should you make provision for all the bills to be paid but don't pay the bill for your time and effort?

The cost analysis of the direct and indirect costs associated with your product or service will guide you in developing a pricing structure that covers your expenses and leaves room for a reasonable and sustainable profit margin.

Once you have pricing guidelines to work with, the next step should be market research and client segmentation. Define your target audience and segment your clients based on demographics, behaviour and preferences. This is because different client segments may have varying price sensitivities and needs. Once you have a clear understanding of your niche and client segmentation, you can then tailor your pricing and packaging to each segment's expectations and purchasing power. For instance, your product or service can have tiered pricing, bundles or customisation options to effectively cater to different client groups.

When you have a thorough understanding of your target market and niche, competitor analysis is the next step in developing an effective pricing strategy. Assess the competitive landscape and understand what similar products or services are priced at within your industry and niche. Then, you can compare the products and services in the market with your UVP or **unique selling points** (USP) to position your offerings in a way that justifies your pricing.

Based on your competitive analysis and understanding of your USPs, determine how you want to position your offerings. Will you position yourself as a premium provider with higher prices but exceptional quality or will you focus on affordability and value for money? Your pricing strategy should align with this positioning. Always keep in mind that being the cheapest option in the market is not a sure path to success. Remember, as written earlier in the chapter, value perception plays a significant role in how clients receive your product or service.

Regardless of your pricing strategy, it's essential to shape how clients perceive the value of your offerings. If you choose to position yourself as a premium provider, clients should see a clear and compelling value proposition that justifies the higher cost. Similarly, if you focus on affordability, your clients should perceive your product or service as delivering exceptional value for the price. The key is to align your pricing strategy with your brand identity and USPs. Your clients should consistently perceive the value in what you offer. Client satisfaction and effective marketing that clearly communicates your uniqueness will ensure that they see value in your products or services regardless of your pricing strategy.

Clients perceive packaging or bundling as good value for money rather than charging an hourly rate for your services. Offer packages and bundles that can be labelled in several ways; get creative around the packages' names related to your types of products and services. If, for instance, you had silver, gold and platinum packages, then silver is the basic, gold is silver plus more, and platinum is gold plus more. Stack the value as you go from silver to gold and gold to platinum. If the gold package is 20% more expensive, then make sure it has 40% more value.

Always add value. For example, a complimentary annual membership to your business online club. Create a suite of three to four packages of your services, with each package having four to six components that clients can choose from.

Offer different options, consider a payment plan for your larger-size packages, and consider the use of platforms such as Afterpay and Zip Pay.

One of my top tips is to avoid offering discounts on your services. Instead, add value! For example, offer a voucher for a 2-for-1 deal: "Pay for a one-hour business branding session, and get a complimentary 30 minutes" or "Make a booking by the end of June, and you will receive our 20-page ebook on Powerful Logo Ideas That Have Sold Millions" or "Book in two of our services, and get a $50 gourmet food voucher".

You want your clients coming back for more. Discounting cheapens how your services will be perceived. Don't discount just for the sake of drawing in clients; you would more likely get clients who just use any service on a whim rather than quality clients who will remain with you.

When they're making a buying decision, your potential clients have a lot of fears swirling around in their heads. They're thinking, "Will I be wasting my money?" "Is this product or service going to work?" "Is there some kind of catch I'm not seeing?" "Will I feel like a fool for having tried this service?" You calm these fears when your business stands behind what it offers with a solid guarantee.

Don't be afraid to offer a guarantee that's above and beyond what others provide. Offer a money-back guarantee – scary, but if you are confident in what you do and in the benefits you can provide your clients, offering such a guarantee should not be an issue. The primary question is, what can you do to absolutely assure your client that if something goes wrong, you won't abandon them or pretend they never bought from you in the first place? One bad testimonial can become a very rotten egg, so get to the stink before it smells out!

When it comes to your business, you need to think about your wow factor. This can be likened to the McDonald's toy. Ask any parent the cost of a Happy Meal, and they probably don't know; but ask them about the latest toy their child is collecting from McDonald's, and they are bound to know the answer!

Suppose you're an art therapist. You could include an Art Pack or a beautiful art notebook/scrapbook for your new client package, so they can start to doodle and put down their thoughts and ideas from the sessions they have with you. Your added value does not have to be expensive, but consider little extra provisions you can give your clients to create the memory factor so that they become raving fans who recommend other clients to you.

Another example is creating a loyalty program or online club to encourage repeat clients – "Use our services twice over a six-month period, and you get a complimentary product valued at $XXX." This could be done by creating a points system where the type of package bought gives the clients a certain number of reward points, and if they refer other potential clients, they also receive reward points. Your online club or loyalty program does not have to be complicated, but you need to think about how you reward clients for repeat and referral business.

Don't forget to provide exceptional client service that goes beyond expectations. Prompt response to inquiries, personalised assistance and quickly resolving issues can differentiate your brand and keep clients coming back. The importance of exceptional client service cannot be overstated when it comes to how clients perceive the value of your products or services and, by extension, your pricing. Outstanding client service can justify higher prices and set you apart even in a competitive niche or market.

Consider the businesses you regularly visit – the ones you keep returning to – even if they come with a higher price tag. In many instances, you'll discover that the quality of service is a big factor that influences your choice of one business over another. As a client yourself, you have pain points that can guide you in creating a stellar client experience. You know how it feels to have unresponsive suppliers, faulty products and delays in delivery. You can leverage your own experience to create the kind of client experience that adds value to your products and services.

Ultimately, the best pricing and packaging strategy comes down to your unique selling points, client expectations, market dynamics and competitive positioning. By diligently considering these factors, you can craft a pricing strategy that maximises the perceived value of your products and services, ensuring profitability and successful positioning of your business.

WHAT IF

Pricing isn't just about setting numbers! It is about aligning your business with market dynamics, client needs and your own financial goals. Even the best business idea can flop if the pricing strategy is wrong. Some of the downsides of a poor pricing and packaging strategy include:

Loss of profit: A poor pricing strategy can leave you unable to cover your costs and expenses (and that includes paying yourself), resulting in losses and limiting your ability to sustain or grow your venture.

Inability to compete: Pricing that is out of sync with the market can put your business at a competitive disadvantage. You may struggle to attract clients and lose them to competitors with more compelling pricing and packaging strategies.

Perceived lack of value: If clients perceive your prices as too low, they may question the quality or value of your offerings. Conversely, if prices are too high, potential clients may be deterred from purchasing.

Operational challenges: Poor pricing can lead to operational inefficiencies, as you may need to adjust or compromise to maintain low prices or recover from underpricing. This can strain resources and affect service quality.

Stagnation in growth: If your pricing is not quite hitting the mark, it could slow down your plans to expand and move the business forward.

3 ACTION QUESTIONS

1. What are the costs and profit margin of your products and services?

Understanding your operational costs and expenses (that includes you – your salary/wage/drawings) is the first step in crafting a pricing strategy. How much does it cost (direct and indirect costs) to put your product or service on the market? Once you are clear on the costs, the next question is: What is a reasonable profit margin for your product or service that reflects the value of what you are offering? What is the industry average profit margin?

Let's say you're launching an online boutique, selling handmade jewellery and offering jewellery-making e-courses. Your costs include materials, website maintenance, marketing expenses and you (are you getting the message yet? **You!**). After analysing these costs, you determine that each piece of jewellery costs $20 to produce, and you aim for a 50% profit margin. This means that you need to price each piece at $40 to achieve your profit goal.

2. Who is your target audience and what value do they perceive in your products or services?

Understanding your audience allows you to align your pricing with their expectations and willingness to pay. Failure to consider your audience may result in pricing that doesn't resonate with potential clients. For instance, if you are targeting a market segment with different spending power, tiered pricing or bundling helps to avoid alienating a segment of your client base.

Consider whether your pricing strategy caters to the specific circumstances of your target market. For instance, suppose you offer graphic design services for small businesses in a rural area. Your target audience consists of local entrepreneurs with limited marketing budgets. To cater to their needs and budget constraints, you offer a pricing structure that emphasises affordability and value, setting your prices lower than a large urban agency that targets multinational corporations.

3. What are your unique selling points or unique value proposition (UVP)?

By evaluating where you stand relative to competitors in your niche and emphasising what your unique selling points are, you effectively determine how to position your business. Do you fit in the market as a premium provider, value-oriented option or somewhere in-between?

For example, if you are starting a consulting business in a regional area with several established competitors, what are your unique selling points that will set you apart? You can position yourself as a premium consulting or a value-oriented option offering affordability without compromising on the quality of the consulting. In both cases, having a clear UVP is essential for effective pricing and market positioning.

5.

Profit with purpose

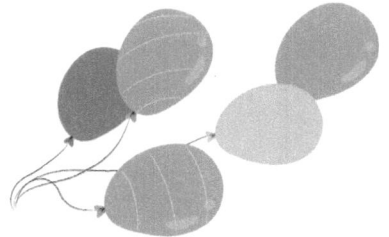

WHY

As an MLPW do you feel the pull to do something more, something that will have an impact and leave a legacy? A pull to give back in some way, serve, encourage and build others? This is how I felt when I began my journey as an MLPW transitioning into self-employment, and I have observed for many other MLPWs that this is the same.

Are you an MLPW on a pathway to recovery from challenging personal experiences – some form of trauma such as adverse childhood experiences, domestic violence, divorce or a cancer journey – determined to rise again and use your adversity for good?

Do you want to leave a legacy and use your adversity for good? One way you can do that is by running your business as a profit-for-purpose. In other words, you are not choosing to start your business solely to generate income – though, this is a necessary part – but there is a more significant factor you want your business to have.

Think about your why and the causes close to your heart. Do you want to promote better environmental policies in your community? What can you do to integrate this purpose into your business model? Do you want to play a role in social causes in your area? How can you integrate social responsibility into your business strategy? Figuring out how your business can have an impact will help you establish a brand that resonates with your target market. This creates a kind of social capital where your business has shared values and norms within the community. This kind of social capital can be invaluable in setting you apart from the competition.

Having a purpose-driven business model is not solely about finances, but it can also be achieved through strategic decision-making. For instance, adopting sustainable sourcing practices that reduce wastage or opting for eco-friendly packaging are strategies that do not necessarily require more capital but still position your business as an entity that cares about more than just profits. Considering your business model and the type of product or service you offer, think of ways that you can align your goal – making money – with a greater purpose.

Fulfilling a great goal will not only have a positive impact on your business but also give you an added sense of satisfaction from knowing that you are making a mark in your community and establishing a legacy. Just remember to balance your community initiatives with remaining profitable. It is easy to get caught up in causes and neglect the other aspect of a successful business – remaining profitable. Your desire to be a profit-for-purpose business can lead you to give away too many of your services for pro bono or on a sliding scale, which can lead to the point where your business becomes no longer financially viable.

For example, let's say you own an interior design business, and you are dedicated to giving back to the community by donating a portion of your profits to local charities. While your philanthropic efforts are admirable, you must strike a balance. If you overcommit to donations without considering your business's financial health, you risk jeopardising your ability to support these causes over the long term. Instead, you might implement a "Give Back Week" initiative, where a percentage of Week 3 sales every month goes to charity, ensuring that your business remains financially viable even as you make a difference in your community.

Ultimately, finding a great purpose that reflects your values, experiences and greater goal will help you create a business that positively impacts your community and makes a meaningful difference in the lives of others and the environment.

WHAT

Profiting with purpose involves running a business or being self-employed in a way that not only generates profits but also aligns with one's values, passions and a larger sense of purpose. It involves integrating a sense of meaning and positive impact into the core of your business operations while also striving for financial success.

Profiting with purpose goes beyond just making money; it involves being intentional about creating a business that has a positive impact on people, communities or the environment while also being financially sustainable. It means using your business as a vehicle for creating positive change and contributing to a greater good beyond just the bottom line.

By profiting with purpose in self-employment, you can create a business that not only generates financial success but also brings fulfilment, satisfaction and a sense of meaningful impact. It allows you to align your work with your personal values and passions while also making a positive contribution to society, which can be personally and professionally rewarding.

HOW

Your approach to creating a business with a profit-for-purpose foundation will determine whether you can balance profitability and having a greater purpose. It is important to start with what you have, and finish as you mean to. This simply means that you should utilise your available resources to accomplish the purpose you have in mind. Instead of looking for additional capital to support your social business or purpose initiatives, start by optimising your existing systems and operations to support the greater goal you want to align your business with.

Let's say, for example, you want to run an ecotourism business. To make your business more sustainable, you can start by implementing practices that minimise your business's ecological footprint, such as discouraging the use of single-use plastic in your tours, educating guests on conservation measures or taking part in environmental conservation efforts. These kinds of initiatives can be seamlessly woven into your daily business activities without negatively impacting your bottom line. This allows you to commit to a cause while still ensuring that your business remains financially viable.

Whether you are offering a product or service, you could implement policies in your daily operations that reflect your greater purpose. For instance, if you want to start a cooking classes business, taking time to learn about sustainable practices such as minimising food waste through composting, using eco-friendly packaging and locally sourcing ingredients to support farmers are simple but effective strategies you can put in place to ensure that your business operations are environmentally and socially responsible.

Remember that the goal of a profit-for-purpose model of business is to align your business with the values and causes that are important to you. This means being authentic in the causes or purpose you choose to commit to. Avoid jumping on bandwagons or getting distracted by shiny objects. This means staying true to the values you hold and not getting distracted by passing trends or the cause of the day. Stay true to your chosen purpose and resist the allure of fleeting opportunities. If you are focused on the long-term impact you want to create, you will be able to distinguish between what's genuinely aligned with your values and what's merely a distraction.

Authenticity builds trust and credibility with your clients, employees and stakeholders. When people see that your commitment to a cause is genuine and unwavering, they are more likely to support and engage with your business. In contrast, if you constantly shift your focus to follow trends or causes of the day, you risk appearing insincere and opportunistic. This can erode trust and eventually damage your brand's reputation. Authenticity requires consistency in your actions and messaging. It means staying dedicated to your chosen purpose over time, even when faced with challenges or setbacks.

Even as you support the causes that align with your values, do not forget to keep track of your spending on social responsibility initiatives. Crunch your numbers regularly to ensure that you are not overspending on causes and see if there is room for you to do more. It may be easy to overlook such costs, especially when it is a cause you are deeply committed to. But remember that just like any other expenses, social responsibility expenses will impact your balance sheet. Regularly tracking your spending involves monitoring the allocation of funds to specific initiatives, assessing their impact and evaluating their cost-effectiveness.

The goal of a profit-for-purpose business is to create a lasting impact. To achieve this, you must ensure your business remains financially sustainable over the long term. This means effective financial management, including tracking spending to ensure that your financial resources are used efficiently and maximising your ability to contribute to causes while maintaining a healthy bottom line. Do not be afraid to pull back and re-evaluate your strategies if they are putting a drain on your resources.

If you are starting out with limited resources, it pays to make the smell of an oily rag your friend! This simply means making the most of available resources to achieve your goals. For instance, if you want to implement environmentally sound practices but do not have the budget yet, how about starting with a simple initiative like opting for digital documentation and recycling whenever possible instead of paper printing? This will not only save your business money in terms of printing costs but allow you to operate in an eco-friendly way.

By efficiently utilising resources, you can allocate more funds and efforts towards social impact initiatives. Regardless of your business set-up or operation model, there are plenty of opportunities to get creative with your profit-for-purpose initiatives, even on a limited budget. Be open to learning and discovering ways to make an impact without necessarily having a huge budget. Making the most of what you have can lead to long-term sustainability and increased impact. By being resourceful, your business can extend its reach and influence within your community and industries. As an added plus, resource-efficiency will boost your business resiliency, ensuring that you can bounce back despite challenges such as economic downturns or supply chain disruptions. A business that has embraced frugality and sustainability will be better prepared to weather the storms that are inevitable in business.

Being economical and resourceful does not imply being miserly or refraining from generosity and investment! Instead, it means making efficient and thoughtful use of resources while recognising the importance of strategic investments and responsible generosity. Being economical means carefully assessing the costs and benefits of decisions. You should evaluate whether an expense or investment aligns with your purpose and long-term goals. For instance, supporting a local community project may require an initial investment but can result in enhanced brand reputation and community engagement.

Profiting for purpose, when done right, can prove to be a powerful tool for engaging your target market and may even pay off in increased revenue for your business. Strong social responsibility contributes to a positive brand image. When your business is associated with positive social or environmental impact, it becomes a lot easier to build brand loyalty and positive word-of-mouth marketing. Clients who feel proud to be associated with your brand will likely become repeat buyers and advocates, leading to increased sales and profitability.

Apart from your client base, supporting profit-for-purpose initiatives is a great way to build partnerships and collaborate with like-minded organisations and groups. These collaborations can be beneficial for networking as well as brand-building. When you collaborate with other stakeholders, you can make a much bigger impact without having to increase your social responsibility expenses. This is because partnerships allow you to pool resources with like-minded organisations and gain access to experts and professionals who are passionate about the same cause. Together, you can achieve more significant outcomes than individual efforts would allow.

To attract partnerships and keep your clients updated on your social and environmental initiatives, it is important to communicate openly about your business's values and greater purpose. This will ensure that clients and stakeholders can associate your brand with your chosen cause or initiative. For example, including a section dedicated to your social responsibility activities and initiatives on your website or social media platforms is a great way to share your story and goals related to your social and environmental objectives. This information will be useful in allowing others to understand what common values you share and how your business is impacting the community.

Ultimately, running your business with a greater purpose beyond profits is an investment that yields long-term returns and strengthens a business's position in the marketplace. Think of it as an investment in social capital that will pay off in the form of a positive brand image, client loyalty and competitive edge in your niche market.

For example, consider for a moment that you decide to start a sustainable skincare business. Your purpose beyond profits is to promote eco-friendly practices and support local communities. This positive stance on sustainability creates a brand image that resonates with eco-conscious consumers. As a result, your business becomes known for its responsible practices. Clients who share those values are not just buying your products; they are supporting a cause they believe in. Over time, these clients become loyal to your brand. With time, your business's reputation for sustainability attracts attention from environmental organisations and government agencies. You become eligible for grants, sponsorships and partnerships that can further your mission and provide additional resources to grow your business. This is an example of how your business's greater purpose can propel you to greater heights, enabling you to fulfil the mission and vision for your venture.

WHAT IF

At their core, businesses exist to make money. However, focusing solely on profits can lead to burnout and dissatisfaction among business owners and employees. A sense of purpose and alignment with values that are important to you not only makes for a better work environment but also acts as an added motivator to keep you going.

Some of the downsides of overlooking the greater purpose of your business include:

Loss of client trust and loyalty: In an era where consumers value social responsibility and sustainability, a business solely focused on profits may be perceived as self-serving and disconnected from societal concerns. This can erode trust and result in clients switching to competitors aligned with their values.

Missed market opportunities: Businesses that prioritise purpose often identify innovative solutions and tap into emerging markets. By not aligning with a greater purpose, your business might overlook opportunities to meet the needs of socially or environmentally conscious consumers.

Difficulty attracting and retaining talent: Many employees, especially millennials and younger generations, seek employers who value social and environmental responsibility. Failing to integrate purpose into your business can make it challenging to attract and retain top talent.

Competitive disadvantage: Businesses that prioritise purpose may gain a competitive edge, especially in industries where social and environmental concerns are significant. Ignoring these factors can put your business at a disadvantage against purpose-driven competitors.

Difficulty in building partnerships: Collaboration with like-minded organisations, NGOs and government bodies can amplify the impact of your business. A profit-focused approach may hinder your ability to establish such partnerships.

3 ACTION QUESTIONS

1. How can you integrate purpose into business operations? What causes or initiatives do you want to support and how can you do it authentically while still maintaining financial viability?

Consider how you can align your products or services with your purpose. It could be by implementing sustainable business practices, supporting social or environmental causes or prioritising ethical and responsible sourcing.

2. How can you authentically communicate your purpose?

Authentic and compelling communication can help build trust, connect with like-minded clients and differentiate your business from competitors. What is the best way to communicate your purpose to your target market, stakeholders and community at large? Consider using your website, social media, marketing materials and other communication channels to share your purpose-driven story, values and impact.

3. How can you measure and evaluate the impact of your business in relation to your purpose?

This could involve tracking **key performance indicators** (KPIs) that align with your purpose, such as social or environmental metrics or client satisfaction. Evaluate how well your business practices are contributing to your purpose and making a positive impact. Use the data and feedback to continuously improve and evolve your business strategies and operations to ensure that you are staying true to your purpose.

6.

Turn your services into products

WHY

As an MLPW, there comes a point in your business journey where you can further grow and leverage your skills and experience by turning your services into products.

Toni is a fitness trainer offering in-person sessions and classes in her town. Her income depends on clients signing up for individual sessions or group classes. In this case, her earning potential is dictated by the number of hours she can work. To explore new avenues of income, Toni decided to leverage her skills and experience to develop products.

She started a subscription-based fitness app that provides access to prerecorded workout videos, nutrition guides and virtual coaching. Users pay a monthly fee to access these resources. By doing this, she has opened her client base to include anyone with access to mobile apps and ensured she can earn passive income even when she is not working. This is an example of how you can turn your service into a product and grow your earning potential by diversifying your income streams.

When you position yourself solely as a service provider, your income potential is limited to the number of hours you can work. This limits your options and can even be risky in case you fall ill or encounter circumstances that affect your ability to work. In our example, if Toni, who is a physical trainer, falls ill for a week and cannot teach her fitness classes, she cannot generate income during that period. However, if she develops a product related to her service, she will still have some income streaming in even when she is unwell. Diversifying your income streams in this way not only increases your earning potential but also gives you safety in case of any eventualities.

Turning your service into a product can also help you grow your business from a local brand to a national and even global brand. As a service provider, your reach may be limited to a specific geographical area or a certain number of clients. However, you gain access to a wider client base with products since they don't require you to be physically present to sell. For instance, if you are a management consultant who offers training seminars to corporations, you can compile your knowledge and insights into ebooks or online courses. This will allow you to offer your expertise to a much bigger audience in a more efficient manner. By turning your service into a product, you will reduce your dependence on one-on-one consultations and increase your client base significantly.

The transition from service provider to product creator can empower you to leverage your expertise efficiently, engage a global audience and establish yourself as a respected authority in your field. As an MLPW, you have accumulated a wealth of knowledge and experience in your field. Packaging these knowledge and skills into products that can be sold repeatedly allows you to reach a larger audience and make a broader impact. This can also position you as an authority in your industry, further enhancing your professional reputation and credibility.

Opportunities for growth are also more accessible when you turn your service into a product. This is because products can offer more scalability compared to a solely service-based business. Scaling a service-based business can be challenging since, in most cases, it requires you to hire additional staff, manage logistics and increase your overhead costs. On the other hand, once you have developed a product, you can sell it to multiple clients without incurring significant additional costs. This allows you to scale your business without the constraints of time or resources, and potentially achieve higher profit margins. For example, if you are a graphic designer, you can create digital templates that can be sold to multiple clients or develop a software tool that automates certain design processes.

Creating products is also a great way to tap into your creativity and ability to innovate. It pushes you to think outside the box to find ways to leverage your expertise and experience and turn it into a product. You can design products that reflect your personal style, vision and ideas, allowing you to differentiate yourself in the market. This can be a fulfilling and rewarding process that allows you to express your creativity and explore new ideas. You can also experiment with different product ideas until you find one that suits your service or expertise best by continuously innovating and adapting to changing marketplace demands.

In today's fast-paced business landscape, it's important to adapt and stay relevant. Creating products can be a way to future-proof your business by diversifying your offerings and keeping up with changing market trends. As client preferences evolve, having products in addition to services can provide you with the flexibility to pivot and meet new demands, ensuring the long-term sustainability of your self-employment venture.

WHAT

As an MLPW, you have undoubtedly acquired a wealth of expertise and skills in your field. In what ways can you leverage this expertise to unlock new opportunities and avenues for growth as you venture into self-employment? Anyone can develop a product, but how you package and format your expertise is what will determine whether you end up with a winning formula.

As a service provider, you already have a target audience for your expertise. This means you can draw on your experience to figure out the kind of products you can develop to address your clients' pain points. For example, if you are a physical trainer, you understand that your clients do not always have time to go to the gym. Thus, offering online classes or at-home workout videos via an app will allow your clients to access your sessions from the comfort of their homes or even when travelling. This expands your client base, increases your income streams and creates opportunities for growth.

By tapping into your creativity and experience, you can create unique products that reflect your expertise and vision. This can be a strategic move to achieve financial stability, scalability and long-term sustainability in your self-employment journey.

HOW

Self-employment not only gives you agency over your business journey, but it also opens opportunities to gain financial freedom and independence. If you have accumulated years of experience and expertise in a professional field, you possess valuable skills that can be leveraged in the marketplace. This means you can transition to self-employment by leveraging your existing skills. However, while this can be fulfilling, it is essential to understand that positioning yourself solely as a service provider can limit your earning potential. This is why it is important to find ways to turn your service into a product.

Turning your service into a product allows you to establish passive income streams. While service-based income relies on the hours you work, products can be sold repeatedly without your direct involvement. Imagine you are a website designer who typically offers custom design services. By creating digital design templates or downloadable resources, you can sell these products online, earning income even when you're not actively working with clients. This passive income adds financial stability and flexibility to your self-employment journey.

Of course, before you can turn your service into a product, you first need to figure out what products you want to sell and how best to package them. This means that the first step is identifying your **unique selling point** (USP). Just like services, products need a USP that will make people want to buy them. So, what will be your USP, and what will set you apart from your competitors? To identify your USP, you need to reflect on your skills, experience, expertise and passion. What makes you special? What do you do differently? What problems do you solve for your clients? Once you have identified your USP, you can use it as the foundation for creating products that showcase your unique strengths.

Once you have clearly defined your USPs, it is essential to determine who you want to target with your product. You need to clearly define your target market based on the product you want to sell and what problem it seeks to solve. Your target market is the group of people who are most likely to benefit from your products and are willing to pay for them.

Defining your target market is essential because it helps you understand your clients' needs, preferences and pain points, which in turn allows you to create products that address those needs effectively. When defining your target market, consider factors such as demographics (age, gender, location), psychographics (interests, hobbies, values) and behaviour (buying habits, online behaviour). Understanding your target market enables you to tailor your products to their specific needs, which increases the likelihood of success.

When you determine your target market, it becomes clear what the right product format for your business is. For instance, if you are a mindset coach, an e-course will allow you to reach your target audience online and offer them prerecorded mindset workout sessions they can access at their convenience. Someone offering training courses would probably opt for ebooks as their product format. The right product format will ultimately depend on your product type, target market and overall business strategy.

Think about how you plan to distribute your products. Digital products are typically distributed online, while physical products may require shipping and inventory management. Choose a format that aligns with your distribution strategy. Before you settle on a product format, assess the profit potential of different formats. Some products may have higher production costs but offer excellent profit margins, while others, such as ebooks or online courses, may be low-cost with high sales volume potential.

Embrace digital tools and platforms for content creation and distribution. Invest in creating a user-friendly website or ecommerce platform that will allow clients to access your products with ease. Digital delivery methods, such as email links, downloadable files or access through a membership portal, are also convenient and relatively easy to set up. Remember that there is no one-size-fits-all product format and that the best solution will depend on the nature of your business and your goals.

Some common product formats include:

> **eBooks:** If you have a wealth of knowledge to share, you can create an ebook that provides valuable insights, tips and strategies related to your expertise. eBooks are easy to create and can be sold on online platforms such as Amazon Kindle, Apple iBooks or your website.

Online courses: Online courses are a popular format for turning services into products. You can create a comprehensive course that teaches your target audience specific skills or knowledge related to your expertise. Online courses can be hosted on platforms such as Udemy, Teachable, LearnDash, Thinkific or on your own website.

Templates and tools: Another option is to create templates, worksheets or tools that can help your target audience solve a specific problem or achieve a particular goal. For example, if you are a business consultant, you can create templates for business plans or financial spreadsheets. Templates and tools can be sold on your website or through online marketplaces.

Physical products: Depending on your expertise, you may also consider creating physical products that complement your services. For example, if you are a nutritionist, you can create a line of healthy snacks or supplements. Physical products can be sold through your online store or ecommerce platforms such as Etsy or Shopify.

Once you have a suitable product format for your business, it's time to figure out your product strategy. Your product strategy is a roadmap that outlines the products you plan to create, their features and benefits, pricing, distribution channels and marketing plan.

Develop a pricing strategy that reflects the value of your product and resonates with your target market. Research competitors' pricing and consider factors such as production

Turn your services into products

costs, market demand and perceived value. For instance, if you're a marketing consultant, your product pricing could vary based on the complexity and depth of your marketing strategy templates. You could offer a tiered pricing structure with different rates for basic and more advanced templates. This will allow you to target different market segments based on their budgets and specific requirements.

Just like with any service, a marketing strategy is essential for the success of your product. Implement a marketing strategy to promote your newly created product. Leverage online marketing channels such as social media, email marketing, content marketing and paid advertising to reach your target audience. Highlight the unique benefits of your product and showcase how it addresses your clients' pain points. If you offer personal styling services, promote capsule wardrobe modules that cater to various lifestyle ages – for example, corporate newbie, business entrepreneur in her 50s and so on.

Consider how you will offer customer support for your product since it will be integral to ensuring that your clients know how to get assistance in case of any issues. Provide adequate customer support to address inquiries, concerns or technical issues related to your product. Make sure that you offer clear instructions for product usage and how to troubleshoot common problems. Depending on the scale of your operations, consider using a helpdesk or ticketing system to efficiently manage client inquiries.

Your customer support channels will also be an important source of feedback to help you improve your product and pivot to evolving market trends. Encourage client feedback and use it to improve your product. Regularly update and enhance your product based on user suggestions and evolving market needs. For example, if you're a language tutor, refine your online language course based on student feedback and changing language learning trends.

As your product gains traction, explore opportunities to scale and expand. This may include offering additional related products, targeting new client segments or exploring international markets. For instance, if you offer business coaching courses, expand your product line to include business guides for different industries. Be sure to check laws and regulations, especially when expanding into new markets, to ensure you are compliant with all regulatory requirements. Be aware of copyrights, trademarks, data privacy and other regulations that may apply to your product. If need be, consult a legal professional to stay updated on applicable laws.

Don't forget to keep track of your performance and regularly evaluate the success of your product. This will help you to identify what you are doing right, what needs improvement and opportunities for growth. Establish KPIs to measure the success of your product. Tracking metrics such as sales, client satisfaction and user engagement will give you the data you need to make informed decisions and refine your product strategy.

WHAT IF

Choosing not to turn services into products as an MLPW may have potential downsides or challenges, which could include:

> **Limited scalability:** Service-based work typically involves providing one-on-one or customised services

to individual clients, which may limit the scalability of the business. Without products that can be replicated or automated, there may be limitations on reaching a larger audience or generating passive income, which could impact the potential for business growth.

Reduced income potential: Product-based work, such as creating and selling products, may have the potential for higher profit margins compared to service-based work. Without products, you may miss out on opportunities to generate additional income streams or maximise their earning potential, which could impact your financial goals.

Time- and resource-intensive: Developing and managing products, as well as creating and launching a product line, can require significant time, effort and resources, including financial investment, marketing, production and distribution – short-term pain for long-term gain. But choosing not to turn services into products may mean you need to invest more time and effort into providing services directly to clients, which could impact your work–life balance or availability for other activities.

Limited reach: Products can be distributed widely, allowing for a broader client base, while services are typically limited to the clients with whom direct interactions occur. By not turning services into products, your reach may be limited and you may not be able to expand your impact or influence beyond your existing client base.

3 ACTION QUESTIONS

1. What core elements of your services can be converted into a standalone product?

Based on your experience and expertise, identify the skills you can leverage and create a product. It could be a tool, software, physical product or digital resource that can be packaged and sold independently. Consider what your unique selling proposition is and how you can build that into the product you want to offer.

2. What market research do you need to conduct to validate the demand for your productised service?

What clients' needs and pain points are you seeking to address with your product? What are the competitors in your niche offering, and what will set you apart from them in the marketplace? Answering these questions will guide you on your product strategy, including the right product format, pricing, marketing strategy and more.

3. How can you create a scalable and automated system for delivering your productised service?

Consider the operational aspect of turning your service into a product. How will you deliver the product to your intended market? Is it a digital product that can be sold online or a physical product that requires inventory, shipping and other logistics? How can you create a scalable and automated system for delivering your productised service efficiently and consistently? This may involve developing **standard operating procedures** (SOPs), setting up technology platforms and streamlining workflows to ensure smooth product delivery to clients.

ℱ.

Position yourself as a thought leader

WHY

Suppose you are a professional in marketing and have decided to become a self-employed marketing consultant by launching your consultancy. You have a wealth of experience under your belt, but despite your expertise, you still must stand out in a market that can sometimes get crowded with professionals offering similar services. One way to distinguish yourself from the crowd is by positioning yourself as a thought leader in your field. This means positioning yourself as a clear and distinct brand with specific expertise that sets you apart in the marketplace.

For example, to stand out as a marketing consultant with a distinct brand, you could specialise in digital marketing strategies for small businesses in rural areas. You could create case studies highlighting your success in helping local businesses thrive online, showcasing your deep knowledge of the unique challenges they face. This effectively positions you as the trusted expert for rural businesses seeking digital marketing guidance. In essence, you become a brand known for its expertise in marketing for rural businesses rather than just another marketing consultant.

Positioning yourself as a thought leader can have numerous benefits for your personal and professional growth. Being recognised as a thought leader establishes you as an authority in your field of expertise. It positions you as someone who has in-depth knowledge, insights and unique perspectives in your chosen niche, which can attract attention and garner respect from others in your business.

Building a distinct and recognisable brand identity can open doors for opportunities such as speaking engagements, collaborations and partnerships, further enhancing your reputation and credibility. As a thought leader in your field, you get to share your insights and knowledge, which means you can provide value to others and establish yourself as a go-to resource in your field. This can help you build a community of followers who look up to you for guidance and advice, which can lead to increased visibility and influence within your niche. This can help you establish a personal brand that inspires trust with your target audience and creates a lasting impression.

Effective positioning involves identifying a niche, showcasing your expertise or unique qualities and tailoring your messaging and services to cater to a specific audience. This not only helps attract the right clients but also distinguishes you from competitors, ultimately contributing to your success in self-employment. Clients are often willing to pay a premium for services or products offered by recognised thought leaders because of the perception that they are experts in their field. This can lead to increased revenue and profitability for your business, allowing you to scale and explore growth opportunities.

Thought leaders often receive media coverage, speaking invitations and opportunities to contribute to industry publications. This exposure can amplify your marketing efforts and increase brand visibility. For instance, you may be invited to speak at conferences, webinars, podcasts and other events. These speaking engagements can further establish your authority and generate leads for your business.

Regardless of your chosen field, it is possible to position yourself as a thought leader by carving out a niche for yourself based on your experience and specific expertise. For example, if you are an MLPW in the field of education, you might specialise in innovative teaching methods for adult learners. This clearly identifies your area of expertise to your target market and allows you to take a targeted approach by designing your brand and product strategy around the niche you have chosen for yourself. This clarity is invaluable in a competitive landscape where differentiation is key.

By focusing on a particular niche, you can tailor your marketing efforts and product offerings to a specific audience. In our example, your expertise in adult education methods allows you to create content, products and services that directly address the needs and challenges of adult learners. This targeted approach resonates deeply with your target audience, who will feel they are working with an authority they can trust to address their pain points.

Thought leaders are perceived as trustworthy sources of information and solutions. As you share your knowledge and insights within your niche, you build trust and credibility with your audience. This trust is the foundation of strong, lasting relationships with your clients and other stakeholders. This trust is not just beneficial for your brand but also positively impacts your bottom line. Thought leaders often command higher fees for their services, products or consultations, and your expertise in a specialised area can justify premium pricing. You may also attract clients or organisations willing to invest more in your solutions due to your recognised authority.

WHAT

For professional women seeking to exercise creative control over their careers and become financially independent, self-employment can be both rewarding and fulfilling. However, in a competitive market, the ability to distinguish and establish yourself as an authority in your field can have a big impact on how well your venture does. Positioning yourself as a thought leader involves building a strong personal brand, showcasing expertise and consistently providing valuable insights and content to establish credibility and influence within the industry.

Focusing on a niche allows you to dive deep into a specific subject matter and dedicate your resources to that specific niche instead of taking a Jill-of-all-trades approach. For instance,

Dr Natasha, an MLPW, specialises in menopause management through holistic approaches. She offers workshops, online courses and personalised coaching tailored to women seeking natural solutions for menopausal symptoms. Over time, her expertise in that niche continues to grow, and as she acquires a greater depth of knowledge, she can provide unique solutions and insights that can't be easily replicated by others. In this way she has carved a niche out for herself and established herself as an authority and thought leader in her field. This targeted approach is what sets thought leaders apart.

HOW

If you are an MLPW venturing into self-employment, you already have tons of experience and expertise that you can leverage when starting a business. While this expertise will give you the skills and foundation you need for your service or product, you still need a differentiating factor to help you stand out in the marketplace. This is where positioning yourself as a thought leader comes in.

In the competitive world of self-employment, you need a unique and compelling brand identity to stand out and establish yourself as an authority or go-to expert in your niche. But how exactly do you go about positioning yourself as a thought leader in your field? Let's explore how you can go about positioning yourself effectively.

Identify your niche and target audience

Effective positioning starts with having a clear idea of what your niche is and who your target market is. Start by evaluating your professional background, skills, knowledge and areas of passion. What are you genuinely enthusiastic about? What have you excelled at in your career? Your niche should align with your expertise and interests. For example, if you are a marketing professional with a passion for sustainable living, you might consider a niche in sustainable marketing strategies that help businesses promote eco-friendly products and practices.

Once you are clear about what niche you would excel in, it's time to consider its current market trends and demands. Are there gaps or underserved segments? Analyse your competitors and their niches. Look for areas where you can offer a unique perspective or solution. For example, if your niche of interest is the wellness industry, you may find a growing interest in holistic health solutions for middle-aged women, so you focus on holistic wellness coaching for this demographic.

Develop a deep understanding of your ideal clients. What are their pain points, needs and desires? Consider how you should package your service or product to suit the specific demographic you are targeting. What are their main problems, and how can you clearly communicate how you can solve them and cater to their preferences? Identify your USP for this demographic. Do you have specific training in that area? Do you have lived experience that relates to what your target audience is going through? Find out what can set you apart from other competitors offering similar services.

Keep in mind that while it's essential to start with a focused niche, you can always expand your offerings over time. Begin with a niche that aligns with your core expertise, and gradually diversify as you gain traction and recognition. For example, if you start with career coaching for midlife professionals, you can later expand into related areas such as personal branding or entrepreneurship support. Be open to adapting your niche strategy as you learn from your audience.

During this foundational step of positioning yourself as a thought leader, do not forget to consider the profitability of the niche you want to focus on. Assess whether a sufficient market size is willing to pay for your products or services. Ultimately, your goal in business is to make money, so the revenue potential within your chosen niche should always be a factor at the back of your mind.

Showcase your expertise

Let's say that you've chosen a niche as a midlife career coach who helps midlife professionals transition into their chosen fields and navigate an ever-changing work landscape. How do you showcase your expertise, build credibility and inspire trust with your target audience? The first step is to ensure your brand's visibility in the marketplace.

A professional website that showcases your services, qualifications and **unique value proposition** (UVP) is crucial for showcasing your expertise. You can create a blog section on your website where you can consistently publish articles that address common challenges faced by your target market. This content will demonstrate your expertise and help with **search engine optimisation** (SEO) to improve your online visibility.

Creating high-quality content is essential in establishing yourself as an expert in your field. Start by creating a content strategy that aligns with your niche and target audience.

What topics are relevant to your business? What are the common questions or challenges your target audience faces? Create content that provides value, educates and inspires your audience. This can include blog posts, articles, videos, podcasts, social media posts and other types of content that showcase your expertise and insights.

Share your unique perspective and insights to differentiate yourself from others in your industry. Be consistent in your content creation efforts, and engage with your audience through comments, questions and discussions to help you build a loyal following and establish yourself as a go-to resource in your industry.

Don't be afraid to seek out opportunities to be a guest speaker on relevant podcasts, webinars or virtual conferences. Sharing your insights on different platforms can expand your reach and credibility. Downloadable resources, like ebooks, that address specific challenges in your niche are also great resources to help you build your brand and credibility as an authority in your field.

Engagement and community-building

Once you have established visibility for your brand, you now have a platform you can use to engage with your target audience and other stakeholders in your industry. Actively engage with your audience on social media platforms relevant to your niche. Respond to comments, questions and messages promptly. Share valuable content, insights and updates to keep your followers informed and engaged. If you're a wellness coach specialising in midlife health, regularly post on platforms like

Instagram and LinkedIn. Share healthy recipes, fitness tips and motivational quotes. Interact with your followers by responding to their comments and conducting live Q&A sessions on topics of interest.

Build an email list of interested subscribers who want to receive updates and insights from you. Send regular newsletters containing valuable content, industry news and exclusive tips to keep your audience engaged. Encourage discussions on your blog posts by inviting readers to share their thoughts and experiences in the comments section. Respond to comments thoughtfully and engage in meaningful conversations with your readers. Engaging with your target market will help you foster relationships and build your reputation as an authority in a community of like-minded individuals who value your expertise.

Networking and collaboration are key elements of thought leadership. Connect with other professionals in your industry, attend industry events, join relevant online communities and participate in discussions and forums. Share your insights, ask questions and engage in meaningful conversations. Collaborate with other thought leaders or industry influencers to co-create content, share each other's content or participate in joint projects. Networking and collaboration can help you expand your reach, learn from others and build mutually beneficial relationships.

Gather feedback and adapt

Feedback is an invaluable resource for assessing your progress and the kind of impact you are making in the marketplace. Encourage your clients, followers or community members to provide their thoughts, suggestions and opinions. Feedback can also be gathered through surveys, direct inquiries, comments or reviews.

Let's continue with the example of the wellness coach who has been hosting virtual wellness workshops for clients. After each workshop, she could send out a post-event survey to participants, asking them to rate the session, share what they found most valuable and suggest topics they'd like to see in future workshops. This feedback helps the coach gauge the effectiveness of her workshops and tailor future content to better meet her clients' needs.

Say you are that wellness coach. Once you have collected feedback, analyse and implement the insights gained. Be adaptable and open to making changes to your strategies, content or services based on the feedback you've received. Positioning yourself as a thought leader is a continuous process of refining your approach to better align with your audience's preferences and expectations. This ongoing cycle of improvement ensures that you stay relevant, responsive and attuned to your audience's evolving needs.

Be consistent

Every interaction that clients and other stakeholders have with your business should reinforce your brand identity. Many business owners go into business with a clear strategy and plan for their brand but, as they navigate the complexities of self-employment and thought leadership, encounter distractions, shifts in their business focus or changing market dynamics. These factors can lead to a gradual erosion of brand identity.

Position yourself as a thought leader

To be successful as a thought leader in your niche, it is crucial to maintain a unified and cohesive brand identity across all aspects of your business. Apart from consistent visual branding, which includes your logo, colour scheme and overall design elements, you should also have a consistent brand voice and tone in your communications, whether in written content, videos or social media updates. This also extends to your content style, including formatting, writing style and content structure. Your brand's voice should align with your niche and appeal to midlife individuals, as it helps in creating a coherent and recognisable brand presence.

Aim to also be consistent in your content schedule. Whether you publish blog posts, newsletters, podcasts or videos, adhere to a regular posting schedule to keep your audience engaged and informed. Consistency in all aspects of your brand ensures that your audience can easily recognise your brand and have a clear idea of what to expect from you. This helps to build your credibility and inspire trust with your audience.

When clients encounter your brand across various touchpoints and consistently experience the values and expertise you offer, they are more likely to view you as an authority and thought leader in your field. This, in turn, fosters loyalty and encourages referrals, contributing to your long-term success as a self-employed professional. Remember, establishing yourself as a thought leader takes time and effort. Be patient and consistent; provide value to your audience. Over time, your expertise, insights and contributions will help you become a recognised thought leader in your industry and set you apart from the competition.

WHAT IF

Failing to position yourself as a thought leader in self-employment can have several potential consequences:

Limited visibility: Thought leadership is about establishing yourself as an authority in your field, someone others look up to for insights and expertise. If you fail to position yourself as a thought leader, you may have limited visibility in your industry, making it difficult to attract clients or collaborators. This can result in missed opportunities for business growth and professional advancement.

Reduced credibility: Thought leaders are seen as credible and trustworthy sources of information and advice. If you fail to establish yourself as a thought leader, it may impact your credibility in the eyes of potential clients and partners. This can make it challenging to build trust and establish meaningful relationships, which are crucial in self-employment.

Lack of differentiation: Thought leadership helps you stand out from the competition by showcasing your unique perspective and expertise. Without positioning yourself as a thought leader, you may blend in with the crowd and struggle to differentiate yourself from others in your field. This can make it difficult to command higher rates, attract premium clients or win lucrative opportunities.

Missed opportunities for growth: Thought leaders often have access to a wider network of opportunities, such as speaking engagements, partnerships, collaborations and media exposure. Failing to establish yourself as a thought leader may result in missed opportunities for growth and expansion, as you may not be top of mind when such opportunities arise.

Limited influence: Thought leaders can shape conversations, trends and opinions in their industry. If you fail to position yourself as a thought leader, you may have limited influence over your field, which can hinder your ability to make a meaningful impact, create positive change or drive innovation.

3 ACTION QUESTIONS

1. How can you consistently create and share valuable content to showcase your expertise in your field?

Creating and sharing valuable content is essential to establish yourself as a thought leader. You can create content through various channels such as writing articles, publishing blog posts, creating videos, recording podcasts or delivering presentations.

Focus on providing valuable insights, practical advice and solutions related to your expertise. Consistency is key, so develop a content creation plan and schedule to share your expertise with your target audience regularly.

2. How can you actively engage and collaborate with your audience to build meaningful relationships?

Engaging with your audience is crucial in building trust and credibility as a thought leader. Respond to comments and questions on your content, social media posts or other platforms where your target audience congregates. Show genuine interest in their concerns and be responsive. Additionally, seek opportunities to collaborate with your audience, such as joint projects or co-creating content. This will help you build meaningful relationships and foster a loyal following.

3. What speaking opportunities can you seek out to share your expertise and position yourself as a thought leader?

Speaking engagements provide a platform to reach a larger audience and establish yourself as an authority, and speaking at industry events, workshops or webinars can greatly amplify your thought leadership. Look for relevant speaking opportunities in your field and proactively submit proposals or express your interest in speaking engagements. Prepare compelling presentations that showcase your expertise, and be ready to share practical insights and actionable advice.

8.

Create footprints online and offline

WHY

What footprints will your business make? Or, if you have already made the leap into being self-employed, is your business making footprints? Footprints are important – they leave a mark! They represent your business's visibility, reputation and impact in the marketplace. These footprints are made by the visible and traceable marks or impressions your business leaves behind across various platforms, both online and offline. Footprints are essential in building your brand, engaging with your target audience and measuring the impact of your business's actions.

Let's take the example of a freelance Human Resources Specialist. As part of her portfolio, the specialist showcases her previous work on her business website. This ensures that once a potential client visits the website, they can go through the specialist's offerings and evaluate her experience and expertise. She also maintains active profiles on platforms like Facebook and Instagram, regularly posting high-quality samples of her work to showcase her expertise and sharing tips and other content to establish herself as an expert in her field. In addition to the online footprints, the specialist distributes eye-catching brochures around town, providing information about her services for small businesses and other niche markets. All these activities help to build online and offline footprints that contribute to the brand's reputation and competitive edge in the marketplace.

Do you have a strong online presence, including a professional website and active social media profiles? In a competitive market, being found easily can make a substantial difference. Your footprints ensure that people looking for services or products in your niche can discover your business. It also conveys that you are a legitimate and established business professional. This credibility is especially valuable if you are a midlife professional transitioning from traditional employment to self-employment.

When starting out, it is essential to have a strategy for your online and offline footprint. What impression do you want to make with your brand? How will you stand out in a crowded marketplace? How will you leverage your footprints to increase your revenue potential by attracting more clients to your business?

Create footprints online and offline

Start by having a clear idea of what you want your brand to represent. Are you known for quality, affordability, innovation or community involvement? Your brand identity should align with your values and resonate with your target audience. For example, if you're running a marketing consultancy, your brand identity might revolve around helping small businesses market their services and attract new clients. Your online presence should, therefore, showcase these values through engaging content about marketing strategies for small businesses, establishing yourself as an authority in that specific niche.

Remember that the first impression clients will have of your business is through the online and offline footprints your business makes. GE Capital Retail Bank's 2019 Shopper Research Study found that just over 80% of clients research businesses online before buying or visiting a physical address. This means that the decision to purchase is often made even before the client gets to personally interact with your business, so the impact of your footprints will be a major determining factor in how successful your brand is.

Imagine you're an MLPW starting a consulting business, specialising in life coaching and personal development. You have put a lot of effort into developing your coaching programs and want to create a brand that resonates with individuals seeking personal growth and transformation, so you take a targeted approach to ensure that your potential clients know what your brand stands for and what your UVP is.

For your online footprints, you invest in a well-designed website that not only showcases your coaching services but also tells the story of your brand and the positive impact you've had on clients' lives. You also set up a strong presence on social media platforms, like LinkedIn and Instagram, sharing valuable content about personal development, success stories from your clients and your commitment to helping individuals reach their full potential.

Offline, you host local workshops and seminars on topics like goal setting, stress management and achieving work-life balance. These events not only demonstrate your expertise but also create a sense of community around your coaching brand. You also provide free resources, like ebooks and webinars, that address common challenges people face, further establishing your authority in the field. Your branding materials at these events reflect your commitment to personal growth and empowerment, reinforcing your dedication to helping clients transform their lives.

As a result of these well-planned online and offline footprints, you create a clear impression of what your brand stands for, making it easy for clients who share your values to easily connect with your brand. You also reach a broader audience since your brand is visible, both online and offline, meaning that people recognise it as the go-to expert. In this way, your footprints help you create a strong and consistent brand identity that positions your business to succeed in a competitive market.

WHAT

Creating the right footprints involves focusing on specific aspects of your business. The first aspect should be your brand identity and messaging. Consider what your brand identity and messaging convey about your business's values, mission and UVP. What do you want clients to think and feel when they see your brand?

The second aspect you should focus on is your online presence. Do you have a professional website that clearly represents your brand values, mission and UVP? Are you utilising social media platforms to engage with your client base and establish visibility for your brand? Your online presence has a huge impact on the visibility, perception and credibility of your brand. The right strategy can garner you a huge audience for your products or service and establish you as an authority figure in your niche.

Finally, consider whether your brand is making an impression offline. Do you attend industry events, join local business organisations and engage with your community? Have you hosted workshops or participated in events that help you showcase your brand and what it stands for? This kind of networking and community involvement is crucial for creating offline footprints.

HOW

A few years back, I went on a holiday with a girlfriend to Sydney. We had some great fun together. I certainly gained lots of insights on client service as we wined, dined and shopped our way around Sydney. I was so looking forward to chilling out with a facial and getting my nails painted, but the beauty therapist seemed uptight and a little stressed.

"How are you doing?" I asked.

"Not good", was her reply, and then she went on to explain to me that she had just split with her partner the night before and was now trying to juggle the business and had to quickly take breaks to rush back to day care to breastfeed her one-year-old child!

I felt for her, as I know what it can feel like in very difficult times (as we all can from our various life experiences), but she did not stop talking about her situation for the whole appointment! Consequently, I came out of the appointment feeling very heavy-hearted rather than uplifted and energised.

> INSIGHT: Don't share your current "crisis" with your client unless the context of your products or services and familiarity and knowledge of your client make it appropriate to do so!

Always keep in mind that the interactions you have with your clients influence how they perceive your brand. Although what happened to me was not necessarily bad, the oversharing during the appointment diminished my experience by leaving me feeling downhearted – certainly not the feeling you want your client to walk away with from your premises. As you engage and connect with your clients, do not forget that the impression you make as a businessperson impacts the perception of your brand, whether consciously or subconsciously. It pays to be aware of the kind of impression you create, even when it's just a casual conversation. Remember, footprints are not solely created on purpose; sometimes it is the things you do when you are not paying attention that will leave a lasting impression about your brand.

Apart from client interactions, always ensure that your brand messaging is consistent with what you offer. This is crucial for credibility and building trust with your clients. If there is a disconnect between your brand messaging and what you deliver, you risk your brand integrity.

For instance, using a voucher I bought online, I booked into a restaurant that was advertised as "overlooking Darling Harbour". At first, we had difficulty finding the restaurant and had to ask another eatery along the way – yes, there was a sign to the restaurant, except it was covered up by the positioning of plants and foliage along the front outside the dining area. This foliage also completely blocked out any potential views of the harbour – and on asking for a view, the waiter suggested I could position the table at an angle so that I could see through the small gap in the foliage! So, the view was poor, but I have to say that the seafood platter was simply scrumptious and looked exactly like the picture on the voucher!

> INSIGHT: Be careful how you describe your products and services. Clients get disappointed when a product or service does not meet the expectations and benefits you have set out in your marketing materials. Don't cover up the best "benefits" of your business with "foliage", as it were; have the benefits boldly on display for all to see!

As you set out to establish your online and offline footprints, client feedback will be an invaluable asset in helping you evaluate how your brand strategy is working. Always encourage clients to leave testimonials and reviews on your website and social media platforms. Real-life experience from other clients has a big impact on how potential clients perceive your brand. If your digital platforms include reviews from other clients, it provides potential clients with the evidence that they can trust your brand. It also helps create a good impression, even before the client interacts with your business.

However, client feedback can have its downsides, too, because even when your service or product is stellar, it is impossible to please everyone. For instance, a friend and I had a fun time riding the Sydney hop-on, hop-off bus and took advantage of sitting on the top deck with the wind blowing in our hair and our cameras poised to click at the various points of interest as we rode along. All was going well until a couple joined the bus and chose to sit behind us – oh my goodness, I have never heard anyone complain so much, including the comment "This tour is not good today because it is too windy"! *Move to the lower cover deck* and *Do the tour another day* were my instant thoughts, all while my friend held tight to my arm so that I would not turn around and say my thoughts out loud!

> INSIGHT: No matter what you do, you are **never** going to be able to please all your clients – this is a very hard lesson in business. But the key is to get repeat and referral business from the "lovers" of your products and services rather than from those who choose to critique every little aspect of your business despite how much you go out of your way to make it a pleasurable experience for them.

While your online and offline footprints will be crucial in getting you the visibility and brand recognition you need, the power of client experience cannot be overstated. The way you interact with your clients can be the biggest arsenal in your marketing toolbox, or your biggest liability. A good experience can easily override any negative impression a client may have had about your business. Unfortunately, the reverse is also true – a negative experience will erode any positive impression you have created through your offline or online footprints. Always strive to ensure that clients' interactions with your business consistently align with your brand's values and client expectations. This should start from the very top, with you as the business owner, and trickle all the way down to delivery guys and every other staff that meets your clients.

As you know, a holiday is not a holiday without shopping – in particular, on this Sydney gal's holiday, we went on the hunt at Paddy's Market for a handbag for my friend. We had lots of stalls to choose from, but the client service was certainly not up to par. One assistant looked so hassled when we asked to look at some bags on the top hooks; another, engrossed in reading her magazine and chewing gum, just said no to every question we had; then there was a zealous salesman at one store who grabbed my arm, shoved some handbags in my face and pointed out he had "special prices" just for me, even though I was not the one actually wanting to buy a handbag!

> INSIGHT: Know who your client is; don't assume! Don't look at your clients as if they have dollar signs in their eyes. Take time to get to know your client. Listen to their responses. Check their previous experience or entry level for your product. This was the first handbag my friend ever bought, so she wanted time and space to view lots of samples before making the final choice.

The combination of your business's footprints, good client experience and willingness to adapt to changing market demands will help you stay relevant and competitive in your industry. If you are not sure how to go about the right footprints for your business, here are the areas you should focus on to help build your brand visibility and create lasting footprints:

Online footprints:

Website: Invest in a well-designed website that not only showcases your products but also tells the story of your brand. The site is optimised for local SEO, ensuring it ranks well when people in your area search for your service or products.

Social media: Establish a strong presence on social media platforms, like Instagram and Facebook, sharing visually appealing content about your products, their benefits and your commitment to sustainability. Engage with your followers, respond to comments and encourage user-generated content by reposting client reviews and photos.

Online reviews: Actively seek reviews from satisfied clients, and display them prominently on your website and social media. Potential clients see glowing testimonials about your products' quality, effectiveness and eco-friendliness.

Offline footprints:

Local engagements: Participate in local activities and events, such as local farmers' markets and craft fairs, to showcase and sell your products, and have your booth feature signage and displays that emphasise what your brand stands for and its USP.

Local branding: For businesses serving a specific geographic area, develop offline footprints like physical storefronts, signage and brochures that are consistent with your brand identity and clearly communicate your vision and mission.

Community workshops: Organise workshops in your area on topics relevant to your brand and niche. These workshops not only demonstrate your expertise but also foster a sense of community around your brand.

Packaging: Your product packaging reinforces your brand's identity and values. Include information about your brand's commitment to shared values, such as sustainability, to further indicate what your business stands for.

Online and offline footprints work together to create a holistic brand image for your self-employed venture. They complement each other in helping you build trust and recognition for your business. An active online presence can drive offline traffic, and in-person interactions can lead to increased online engagement. Online and offline footprints leave a mark, build trust and help you reach your target audience effectively, whether you're a digital entrepreneur or a local service provider.

WHAT IF

There are brands you may have never purchased from or directly interacted with, yet you still have a preconceived impression of what they stand for and who they are. This is because offline and online footprints created by brands are the first point of interaction between a brand and its potential clients. This underscores the need to pay attention to the footprints your brand leaves both online and offline. If you overlook the importance of footprints, your venture could face the following downsides.

Inconsistent brand image: Without a clear strategy, your brand image may become inconsistent, confusing potential clients and making it difficult for them to understand what your business stands for.

Lost opportunities: Inconsistent footprints may result in missed opportunities to effectively engage with your target audience. Potential clients may not recognise or remember your brand, leading to lost sales and revenue.

Competitive disadvantage: In a competitive market, businesses with strong, consistent footprints tend to stand out and attract more clients. Inconsistency can put you at a disadvantage compared to competitors with a cohesive brand presence.

Wasted resources: Without a clear strategy, you might invest time and money in marketing efforts that don't align with your brand or resonate with your target audience. This can lead to wasted resources and ineffective marketing campaigns.

3 ACTION QUESTIONS

1. How will your online and offline messaging clearly communicate who you are and what you stand for?

Define your brand identity, values and the message you want to convey to your target audience. Understand what sets your brand apart from competitors and how you want your audience to perceive you.

2. Who is your target audience?

Identify and understand your target audience's demographics, preferences and purchasing behaviour. Knowing your audience helps you to tailor your messaging and choose the right platforms for engagement so that you can effectively reach your audience online and offline.

3. What channels and platforms will you utilise?

It's important to determine which online and offline channels and platforms are most effective for reaching your target audience, depending on your brand and type of product or service. Consider factors like social media platforms, physical locations, events and partnerships that align with your brand message and resonate with your audience.

9.

Multiply your income streams

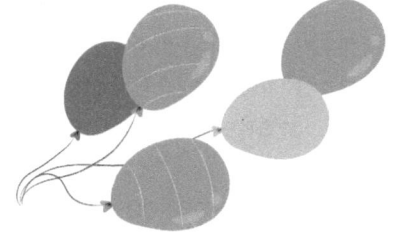

WHY

You could be having a great year revenue-wise, but then an unforeseen circumstance shakes up your business, and you are left staring at losses. Unforeseen circumstances in your personal life, such as suffering an illness, can also seriously impact your finances. While in most cases you do not have control over such situations, you can create a financial safety net for yourself by diversifying your income streams.

Multiplying your income streams refers to diversifying your sources of revenue by increasing your portfolio of services or products, branching out into a different category of services or expanding your reach into new markets. This approach helps to ensure that you reduce over-reliance on a single source of income and create additional opportunities for earning money.

Let's say you are a career coach offering one-on-one coaching to college students seeking to identify the best career path. To diversify your income stream, you start taking on speaking engagements at universities and colleges near you. You also decide to start writing an ebook, sharing your insights as a career coach. During slow coaching seasons, revenue from your ebook and speaking engagements can offset the drop in coaching income, ensuring a steadier overall income. In this scenario, you have gone from a single-income stream to having three streams of income. This is how the concept of diversifying your income streams works.

Multiplying your income streams can be valuable for several reasons. Relying on a single source of income can be risky in today's fast-paced and dynamic economic environment. Market downturns, job lay-offs and new technology are just some of the factors that can upend the business environment and leave you in a less-than-desirable position. When you have more than one income stream, you create a sort of financial cushion that will act as your safety net in case of unexpected changes in your business.

Imagine you're a financial consultant who provides one-on-one advisory services. In the event of you falling ill for a while, your source of income will dry up for the duration you are unable to work. This is because your business requires you to provide one-on-one services. In such a case, if you do not have an alternative source of income to fall back on, you may find yourself in very difficult financial circumstances. However, if, for example, you also offer online courses or ebooks, you would still have a source of income to keep you going until you can resume your one-on-one advisory services.

Apart from providing you with a financial safety net, having multiple income streams increases your earning potential by increasing your service or product portfolio and market base. For instance, if you offer ebooks or online courses along with your other services, you can effectively reach a much wider audience, which means more opportunities to generate revenue. If you are offering in-person services, like coaching, your reach will be limited to a certain geographical location, but with the addition of digital products to your portfolio, you immediately expand your reach to national and even global markets.

Multiplying income streams can provide flexibility and freedom. You can create passive income streams that can generate revenue for you without requiring your presence. This will not only give you more control over your work-life balance but also allow you to pursue your other passions. This can lead to greater personal satisfaction and improved quality of life. Consider an MLPW who has been running a successful coaching consultancy for several years. While she enjoys her work and the income it generates, she's increasingly aware of the toll it takes on her personal life. She's missing out on family gatherings, her favourite hobbies and simple moments of relaxation.

It's not unusual to become disillusioned with your career or business because of the toll it takes on your personal life. Having a business or job that drains the life out of you can be the exact opposite of the life you pictured for yourself, especially if you are a midlife professional looking to travel, spend time with family and enjoy other pursuits besides work. This is precisely why establishing a passive income stream can be one of the most liberating decisions you make for yourself. Passive income allows you to earn money with minimal ongoing effort, providing you with the freedom to enjoy life beyond work-related obligations.

Exploring other avenues of income is also a great way to tap into opportunities you have not explored before. For example, think about the thrill of having a bestseller in global marketplaces like Kindle. Suddenly, people in places you have never even visited are reading and enjoying your work! Apart from earning more income, you can learn more about your skills and expertise by exploring new opportunities and finding new ways to leverage your skills. The more you push yourself to repackage and diversify your streams of income, the more likely you are to discover new talents, skills and strengths you have never tapped into before.

The more income streams you have, the more revenue you can generate from your venture. Having multiple income streams will contribute to your long-term financial goals. It will help you build savings, plan for retirement or invest for the future. This not only helps you meet your financial goals but also ensures your financial stability and security in the long term.

WHAT

Multiplying your income streams does not have to be complicated. A great place to start is always with what you have. So, what can you do with your current resources and expertise to open a new income stream? If you are a freelance ghostwriter taking gigs from clients, what else can you do to diversify your ghostwriting? Can you perhaps write and publish your own books to generate passive income so that you are covered when ghostwriting gigs are not forthcoming? If you offer in-person services like consulting or training, can you develop a digital product, like an online course, as a second stream of income that does not require your constant attention?

Whatever your line of work or expertise is, there are plenty of ways to explore different avenues of income and increase your income potential. If possible, target passive income streams when looking for additional revenue sources, since they will not be time-consuming once they are set up and launched. Remember, diversifying your income streams should not equate to you running yourself ragged, trying to balance 10 things at once. The best secondary income streams complement your existing business without negatively impacting your lifestyle or adding more stress to your plate.

HOW

Diversifying your income streams isn't just a strategy for seasoned entrepreneurs or financial experts – it's an approach that every professional with expertise can leverage to supercharge their financial journey. Whether you're a consultant, coach or freelancer, your skills and knowledge are valuable assets that can be harnessed to create multiple income streams

Imagine you are a midlife professional, a skilled career coach helping others navigate their professional paths. While your expertise is undoubtedly your primary income source, why stop there? By exploring secondary income streams, you can reach your financial goals faster and open exciting opportunities for personal and professional growth. Not to mention, diversification is a powerful wealth-building strategy, setting you on the path to long-term financial security.

Diversifying your income streams can also offer you the chance to develop new skills, connect with a broader audience and create a legacy. Whether you're looking to increase your financial stability, discover fresh challenges or simply achieve a better work-life balance, turning your expertise into several income streams can work together to fuel your dreams.

Of course, before you get started, you will need a strategy for finding the best alternative or secondary sources of income based on your experience, field of interest and resources. The first step should be conducting an honest self-assessment of your skills, expertise and passions. What are you genuinely good at? What do you enjoy doing? For example, if you're a training-and-development professional, you possess a wealth of knowledge in professional development. Perhaps you also have a talent for writing, public speaking or teaching. Any of these skills can be your foundation in establishing another income stream.

Resist the temptation to follow the crowd or chase the latest trends simply because others are doing it. Diversifying your income streams doesn't mean you have to jump on the ebook-writing bandwagon if that's not your forte. Instead, focus on building a solid foundation for your additional income sources based on your expertise and genuine passion. For example, if you're a seasoned financial advisor with a deep understanding of investment strategies and a passion for educating others, offering online investment workshops or personalised coaching sessions might be a better fit than attempting to become a bestselling author overnight.

The key is to leverage what you're genuinely good at and passionate about. This not only enhances your credibility and authority but also makes the effort you put into your secondary income sources feel less like work and more like a fulfilling pursuit. It's about finding that sweet spot where your skills align with market demand and your personal interests. Remember that there are countless ways to diversify your income, and what works for one person may not work for another. While ebooks, online courses or affiliate marketing may be popular choices, you have the flexibility to explore unconventional or less crowded avenues.

Once you have a good idea of the skills you want to leverage and the niche you want to explore, it's time to do some market research. Investigate the market demand for your skills and the services you want to offer. Are there gaps or underserved niches within your industry? Consider the evolving needs of your target audience. If you're a career coach, is there a growing demand for online courses or webinars on topics like remote work skills or personal branding? Identifying how your skills match market needs is crucial for packaging your service and developing a second income stream that is profitable.

When you have a clear idea of how your service fits into the marketplace and how to position yourself, assess your current resources. Assess all the resources at your disposal, including time, finances and existing networks. Some income streams may require more substantial investments than others. For instance, launching an online course might involve upfront costs for course development and marketing, whereas freelance consulting might have fewer financial requirements but necessitate an extensive professional network.

Don't forget to consider the time demands of the venture you want to pursue. If you are already working 10 or more hours a day, taking on an additional time-consuming venture may be counterproductive. Remember that resources are not just the capital or money you need to put into the venture; time and effort also need to be weighed carefully before you take the plunge.

You can start small and test the waters with your new service. This tryout phase will give you a chance to gauge market response and adapt your strategy based on results. As you gain experience and confidence, you can then consider scaling up if the income stream is successful and showing potential for good returns. If, on the other hand, you do not seem to be making headway, you can try re-strategising or going back to the drawing board until you find an income stream that is profitable.

It may be tempting to explore multiple income streams at a go, but while this may work in some cases, it is more prudent to launch one product or service at a time. This will give you ample time to measure and assess its performance before adding on another product or service. Remember, the goal is to find a long-term stream of income, even if it means gradual growth, rather than to start on a high and then crash and burn. Simultaneously launching multiple income streams can be overwhelming and challenging to manage effectively, so take a gradual, step-by-step approach that allows you to build a robust foundation for each income stream, reducing the risk of burnout or misallocation of resources.

Multiply your income streams

While the best secondary sources of income for you will largely depend on your expertise and area of interest, there are some common strategies that are effective for most midlife professionals with a wealth of experience in a particular field. These include:

Diversifying your services/products: If you offer a single service or product, consider expanding your offerings to diversify your income streams. For example, if you're a marketing consultant primarily serving clients in the tourism industry, a downturn in tourism due to unforeseen events (e.g., a pandemic) could significantly impact your income. However, if you diversify your services to include other sectors like healthcare or technology, you're better insulated against industry-specific fluctuations.

Target multiple markets/audiences: Expanding your target market or audience can open new income streams. Consider identifying additional niches or segments that can benefit from your services or products, and tailor your marketing efforts towards them. For example, if you are only offering in-person services, how about expanding to online consultations and reaching markets outside your current geographical area?

Create and sell digital products: Develop content that remains relevant over time. Evergreen content, such as blog posts, YouTube videos or guides, can generate passive income and may not be as time-consuming as in-person services or products.

Offer consulting or coaching services: If you have expertise in your field, consider offering consulting or coaching services to other individuals or businesses. You can charge a premium for your knowledge and experience, and it can be an additional income stream alongside your primary business.

Collaborate with other professionals: Collaborating with other professionals in complementary fields can create new income streams. For example, if you are a web designer, you can collaborate with a copywriter to offer comprehensive packages to clients. This not only increases your appeal to clients who prefer to work with a single contractor but also effectively diversifies and increases your income potential.

Leverage online platforms: Take advantage of online platforms, such as ecommerce marketplaces, freelancing websites and social media, to expand your reach and generate income from multiple sources. Utilise these platforms to showcase your services or products, connect with clients and increase your income potential.

Improve your skills and expertise: Continuously improving your skills and expertise in your field can lead to higher rates or fees, better opportunities and increased demand for your services or products. Stay updated with industry trends, invest in professional development and continually refine your offerings to attract more clients and increase your income streams.

Multiplying your income streams requires effort, dedication and strategic planning. It may take time to see significant results, so be patient and persistent in your endeavours. Manage your time effectively and avoid spreading yourself too thin. Focus on quality and value in your offerings to build a solid reputation and generate sustainable income streams.

WHAT IF

Failing to multiply your income streams in self-employment can have several consequences, including:

Limited earning potential: Relying solely on one income stream can limit your earning potential. If that one income stream dries up or slows down, it can lead to financial instability and difficulty meeting your financial goals.

Higher risk of financial loss: Relying on a single income stream can also increase your risk of financial loss. If that income stream fails or encounters setbacks, you may have little to fall back on, leading to financial stress and potential financial loss. For example, if your main client goes out of business or the market for your product or service declines, it can significantly impact your income.

Lack of professional growth: Diversifying your income streams often requires exploring new opportunities, developing new skills and expanding your network. By failing to do so, you may miss out on opportunities for professional growth and development, which can impact your long-term success and earning potential.

Increased stress and burnout: Relying solely on one income stream can lead to increased stress and burnout. If that one income stream requires a significant amount of time and effort, it can result in an unhealthy work-life balance and overall wellbeing.

3 ACTION QUESTIONS

1. How can you leverage your existing skills and expertise to offer additional services or products that can generate new streams of income?

By identifying additional services or products that align with your skills and expertise, you can tap into new markets or offer complementary services to your existing clients. For example, if you're an events specialist with expertise in event risk assessment plans, you could diversify your income streams by offering an online course on creating event risk assessment plans for small to medium-sized events.

2. What opportunities are available for diversifying your income streams by exploring different platforms or marketplaces to sell your products or services?

If you are a graphic designer, you could consider selling your designs on multiple online marketplaces or creating an online course to teach your skills. Exploring different platforms or marketplaces can expose your products or services to a wider audience, potentially leading to increased sales and revenue. It also helps reduce dependence on a single platform, mitigating the risk of changes in policies or algorithms that may impact your income.

3. How can you collaborate or partner with other self-employed individuals or businesses to create joint ventures or mutually beneficial projects that can generate additional income streams?

Collaborating or partnering with others can open new opportunities and reach new audiences, resulting in additional income streams. By pooling resources, expertise and networks, you can create synergistic projects that can generate more revenue than what you could achieve individually. For example, if you are a fitness coach, you could collaborate with a nutritionist to offer a combined fitness and nutrition program.

10.

Design a signature system

WHY

Your signature brand represents your unique identity, expertise and the value you offer to your target market. It is more than just a logo or tagline; it encompasses your personal and professional brand story. Creating a signature system can be a game changer for self-employed entrepreneurs, providing them with a unique and powerful tool to establish their brand, differentiate themselves in the market and achieve greater success in their businesses.

Here are some of the reasons why you should have a strategy for designing a signature system for your business:

A signature system helps with branding and differentiation.

In today's competitive self-employment landscape, it's essential to stand out from the crowd. Having a signature system allows you to define your unique approach, methodology or process for solving a specific problem or meeting a particular need in your industry. This sets you apart from your competitors and helps you create a memorable brand that resonates with your target audience.

For example, if you are a Grief and Loss Counsellor, your UVP might be centred on your deep understanding of the challenges faced by midlife professionals seeking to work through divorce and separation. You can highlight how your own journey through this challenging season has led to valuable insights that can benefit your clients facing the same circumstances.

A signature system brings consistency and efficiency to your business.

When you have **standard operating procedures** (SOPs) for your processes and operations, you build consistency in results, which ensures that you deliver high-quality services to your clients all the time.

Having SOPs also saves you time and resources in addition to ensuring the consistency you need to inspire trust in your target market. When your client knows exactly what to expect from you every time they come to you for a service, they are more likely to be loyal. For example, if you are a freelance website designer, having a standardised process to handle client requests, create design briefs and follow website guidelines maintains consistency in the design quality you offer, so clients can engage you with confidence since you always deliver the same quality of service.

A signature system offers scalability and replicability.

A well-designed signature system can be scaled and replicated, enabling you to serve more clients without compromising quality. It can be a foundation for expanding your business, training team members or even franchising your self-employment model.

This scalability allows you to leverage your expertise and grow your business in a strategic and sustainable way. For instance, if you have established SOPs in your business, onboarding new employees becomes a lot easier since there is a system in place that ensures everyone on your team is working from the same script.

A signature system adds value to your clients.

It provides them with a clear and structured approach to solving their problems or meeting their needs. This helps them understand the value of your offerings and gives them confidence in your abilities. When your clients see that you have a proven system in place, they are more likely to trust you and invest in your products or services. It also enhances the overall client experience, leading to client satisfaction, repeat business and positive referrals.

A well-implemented signature system has the potential to increase your income.

As it represents your unique expertise and approach, you can position your services or products as premium offerings and command higher prices in the market. Clients are often willing to pay a premium for specialised and proven solutions. This can significantly impact your bottom line and increase your income potential, resulting in improved profitability for your self-employed business.

Ultimately, having a signature system enhances your professionalism and credibility as a brand. It inspires confidence from your clients and positions you as an expert and a recognised authority in your industry, enhancing your professional image and credibility. This can lead to a stronger business reputation, which in the long run contributes to your business's success.

WHAT

Designing a signature system is the process of developing a unique and cohesive framework or approach for delivering a particular service, product or solution in a consistent and recognisable manner. Your signature system should revolve around the core service or expertise you offer. Consider how you can structure your services in a unique and valuable way. For instance, continuing the example of a career coach, you might develop a signature system that includes personalised career assessments, goal setting, tailored action plans and ongoing support. This system not only demonstrates your expertise but also offers a structured approach that clients can rely on for tangible results.

The second aspect you should consider when crafting a signature system that helps you standout is building a memorable client experience. Your signature system should prioritise client satisfaction and engagement. For example, if you're a freelance Primary Education Curriculum Specialist, your system might involve a well-defined process for understanding client preferences, regular progress updates and post-project follow-ups to ensure the client's vision aligns with the final product. This client-centric approach enhances your brand reputation and encourages repeat business and referrals.

HOW

In this era of heightened consumer expectations and increased competition, having a signature system boosts your credibility and helps you attract and retain a loyal client base. At its core, a signature system represents your brand's identity and expertise, offering a clear value proposition to potential clients. It showcases your distinct approach to problem-solving and demonstrates your commitment to delivering tangible outcomes.

In an age where consumers are inundated with choices, a well-crafted signature system acts as a beacon, guiding clients to you as the trusted expert in your niche. It simplifies clients' decision-making process by highlighting what makes your services unique and how they can benefit. For midlife professionals venturing into self-employment, a signature system can be a lifeline in a crowded marketplace. It provides a structured framework for consistently delivering exceptional service, instils confidence in your clients and positions you as a thought leader in your industry.

By following a well-defined system, you not only streamline your workflow but also enhance the perceived value of your offerings. This, in turn, leads to increased client satisfaction, referrals and business growth. So, how can you create your own signature system as a self-employed entrepreneur?

Step 1: Identify your niche and target market

The first step in designing your own signature system is to identify your niche and target market. Your niche is a specific area of expertise or specialisation within your industry, and your target market is the group of people or businesses who would benefit the most from your services or products. By narrowing down your focus, you can better understand the unique needs and pain points of your target market and create a signature system that specifically addresses them.

Start by conducting market research to identify gaps or opportunities in your industry. What are the common challenges or problems that your target market faces? What solutions are currently available, and how can you differentiate yourself from them? Consider your own strengths, experiences and expertise, then align them with the needs of your target market to determine your niche and define your ideal clients.

Step 2: Define your outcome

The next step in designing your signature system is to define the outcome or result that your system aims to achieve. What specific transformation or benefit will your clients experience after going through your system? This outcome should be clear, compelling and aligned with the needs and desires of your target market. It should also be something you can consistently deliver and measure to demonstrate the effectiveness of your system.

For example, if you are a business coach specialising in helping small businesses increase their sales, your outcome could be "Double your sales in 90 days" or "Create a profitable sales funnel that generates leads on autopilot". By defining a clear outcome, you can set expectations with your clients and motivate them to invest in your signature system.

Step 3: Develop your unique methodology

The core of your signature system is your unique methodology or framework. This is the systematic approach you use to deliver the desired outcome for your clients. Your methodology should be based on your expertise, experience and knowledge, and it should set you apart from your competitors. It should be easy to understand, implement and communicate, and it should be flexible enough to be adapted to the unique needs of each client.

Start by brainstorming and organising your ideas into a logical and sequential framework. Consider the steps or stages your clients need to go through to achieve the desired outcome. What are the key concepts, strategies or tools that you use in your work? How do they fit together to create a cohesive system? Once you have a rough outline of your methodology, refine it and give it a unique name or brand that reflects your personal style and expertise.

Step 4: Create your signature materials

To effectively communicate and deliver your signature system, you need to create a set of signature materials that serve as your system's tools, resources and assets. These materials can include written documents, templates, worksheets, videos, audio or any other format relevant to your industry and target market.

Your signature materials should be professionally designed, visually appealing and aligned with your brand identity. They should also be easy to understand, implement and follow, providing clear instructions, examples and illustrations to guide your clients through each step of your system. Your materials should also be adaptable and customisable to accommodate the unique needs and preferences of your clients. By creating high-quality and user-friendly signature materials, you can enhance the effectiveness and value of your signature system and establish yourself as an authority in your industry.

Step 5: Test and refine your system

Once you have developed your signature system and created your signature materials, it's important to test and refine your system to ensure it delivers the desired outcome for your clients. Start by piloting your system with a small group of clients or beta testers and gather feedback on their experience. Did they find your system easy to understand and implement? Did it help them achieve the desired outcome? What challenges or obstacles did they encounter? Use their feedback to identify areas of improvement and refine your system accordingly.

It's also important to continuously update and evolve your signature system as your industry or target market changes. Stay updated with the latest trends, technologies and best practices in your field and integrate them into your system to ensure its relevance and effectiveness. Be open to feedback from your clients, peers and mentors, and be willing to adjust your system as needed to serve your clients better and stay ahead of the competition.

Step 6: Promote your signature system

Creating a signature system is not enough; you also need to effectively promote it to attract your ideal clients. Your signature system can be a powerful marketing tool that sets you apart from your competitors and positions you as an expert in your field. Marketing your signature system is not only about showcasing its value but also about creating a compelling narrative that resonates with potential clients.

A compelling narrative around your signature system explains why and how you developed it, the unique problems it solves and the benefits it offers to clients. Develop content that educates your audience about your signature system and its advantages. This can include blog posts, videos, webinars or podcasts. You can also leverage your existing marketing channels like your website, social media platforms, email marketing and even offline channels to market and promote your signature system.

Step 7: Deliver exceptional results

The success of your signature system depends on the results it delivers for your clients. It's crucial to ensure that you consistently deliver exceptional results to build a strong reputation and generate positive word-of-mouth marketing. Make sure to provide outstanding client service, promptly address any issues or concerns and continuously monitor and measure the effectiveness of your system.

Track and measure the results your clients are achieving through your signature system. Collect testimonials, case studies or success stories from your clients who have benefited from your system, and use these testimonials as social proof in your marketing efforts. Share the outcomes and successes of your clients to showcase the effectiveness of your signature system and encourage potential clients to choose your services.

Be open to feedback from your clients and continuously improve and refine your system based on their needs and feedback. Consider conducting surveys, feedback sessions or evaluations to gather client insights and suggestions on how you can further enhance your signature system. By continuously improving and delivering exceptional results, you can establish a strong reputation as a go-to expert in your field and attract more clients interested in your signature system.

Creating your own signature system may require time, effort and resources, but it can be a worthwhile investment that sets you apart from your competitors, positions you as an authority in your industry and attracts more clients who are interested in your unique offering. By developing a successful signature system, you can take your business to new heights and achieve sustainable success as a self-employed entrepreneur.

WHAT IF

Failing to create your own signature system as a self-employed entrepreneur can have several negative consequences for your business. Here are some potential outcomes:

Lack of differentiation: Without a unique signature system, you may struggle to differentiate yourself from your competitors. This can make it challenging to stand out in a crowded marketplace and attract clients looking for a distinct offering. You may end up competing solely on price or other generic factors, leading to a race to the bottom and lower profit margins.

Reduced expertise perception: Having a signature system can position you as an expert in your field and elevate your perceived level of expertise. Without a clear and structured system, potential clients may perceive you as less knowledgeable or experienced, which can affect their confidence in your abilities. This may result in fewer inquiries, lower conversion rates and difficulty commanding premium pricing for your services.

Inconsistent service delivery: Without a standardised system, your service delivery may lack consistency. This can lead to variations in the quality of service you provide to clients, which can impact their satisfaction and referral potential. Inconsistent service may also result in increased errors, rework and client dissatisfaction, leading to negative reviews or feedback that can harm your reputation.

Missed business opportunities: A well-defined signature system can open various business opportunities, such as speaking engagements, collaborations, workshops and media exposure. Without a clear system, you may miss out on these opportunities to promote your business, expand your network and reach a wider audience. This can limit your growth potential and hinder your business's ability to scale.

Lack of clear marketing strategy: Your signature system serves as the foundation of your marketing efforts. Without a defined system, you may struggle to create compelling marketing materials, value-packed content or targeted messaging. This can make your marketing efforts inconsistent and ineffective, resulting in fewer leads, conversions and revenue.

Reduced client retention: A robust signature system can lead to better client outcomes and satisfaction, which can improve client retention rates. Without a structured system, you may struggle to consistently deliver results, meet client expectations and ensure their success. This can result in lower client retention rates, decreased repeat business and reduced referrals from satisfied clients.

Difficulty scaling your business: A well-designed signature system can streamline your service delivery, making it easier to scale your business. Without a clear system, you may face challenges in managing increasing workloads, maintaining quality standards and replicating your success with new clients. This can hinder your ability to grow your business and may result in missed opportunities for expansion.

Time and resource wastage: Without a structured signature system, you may find yourself reinventing the wheel for each client engagement. This can result in wasted time and resources, as you may need to create custom solutions for each client without a standardised approach. This can also lead to inefficiencies, increased workload and reduced profitability.

3 ACTION QUESTIONS

1. What are your core competencies or specialised skills that you can leverage to create a unique system?

Reflect on your unique strengths, expertise and experience that set you apart from others in your industry. Consider what makes your approach or methodology different and how it can benefit your clients. Identify the key elements that make you unique, and use them as the foundation for your signature system. What are the specific benefits or outcomes your clients can expect from your signature system?

2. How can you align your signature system with the goals, values and preferences of your ideal clients to create a compelling offering?

Who is your target market or niche, and what are their specific needs or challenges? Clearly define your ideal client and their pain points, challenges or goals. Understand their needs, desires and preferences to create a signature system that caters to them specifically. This will help you tailor your system to meet their unique requirements and position yourself as their ideal solution.

3. What are the key steps or components of your signature system that need to be consistently followed for optimal results?

How can you create templates, checklists or tools that can streamline your service delivery and ensure consistency? How can you implement your signature system to ensure it is executed effectively every time?

Develop a systematic approach to consistently delivering your signature system to your clients. This may involve creating step-by-step processes, frameworks or methodologies that streamline your service delivery and ensure consistent results. Document your system in a clear and organised manner, which can be easily followed by yourself or your team, if applicable.

11.

Build momentum in your business

WHY

Imagine your business as a river. When it flows, it teems with life and vitality. But when it stagnates, it becomes a breeding ground for inertia. The truth is, a business that isn't growing is like a river that's stopped moving – it begins to collect debris, lose its clarity and eventually dries up. That's precisely why, as a self-employed professional, you need to be the driving force behind creating momentum in your business. Building momentum in your business is crucial for sustained success. As a self-employed individual, you are solely responsible for driving your business forward, and building momentum can help you achieve your goals and stay ahead of the competition.

Think of momentum as the wind beneath your entrepreneurial wings – it's that invisible force that propels your business forward, powering through obstacles and challenges. Just as a river's flow carves its path through even the toughest terrain, business momentum allows you to cut through the clutter of a competitive marketplace. Whether you're a midlife professional embarking on a new venture or a seasoned entrepreneur, the importance of momentum cannot be overstated. It's the lifeline that ensures your business not only survives but thrives. It can be challenging to establish and maintain momentum when you are working independently, but the benefits are well worth the effort.

Momentum provides motivation and focus, which spurs you on and pushes you to do even more. When you see progress and positive outcomes, it boosts your confidence and inspires you to keep pushing forward. You get a sense of accomplishment and satisfaction from seeing something you built start to grow. As the saying goes, progress is often the best form of motivation; it is evidence that whatever you are doing is working. Having momentum in your business will help you stay focused on your priorities and prevent you from getting distracted or losing sight of your goals.

In a competitive business environment, having momentum can give you an edge over your competitors. When you are consistently making progress, achieving results and building a reputation for your services or products, it sets you apart from others. It signals to potential clients that you are reliable, competent and successful, which can attract more business opportunities. In self-employment, building momentum is essential for establishing your brand, creating a niche for yourself and positioning yourself as a trusted and reputable professional.

Momentum can also significantly impact your productivity and efficiency as a self-employed individual. When you are in the flow of making progress and achieving results, it increases your productivity and effectiveness. You become more focused, driven and efficient in your work, which helps you accomplish tasks and projects more quickly and effectively. Momentum eliminates distractions, minimises procrastination and encourages you to act, leading to higher productivity levels and better business outcomes. Additionally, momentum will help you build a positive reputation for your brand. When your business moves from strength to strength, it signals to your target audience and other stakeholders that you are an expert in your niche and an authority in the industry.

When you consistently deliver on your promises, exceed expectations and achieve results, it establishes a positive perception of your services or products. This can spur word-of-mouth marketing for your business through satisfied clients' testimonials and positive reviews, further enhancing your reputation and attracting more business. A positive reputation is crucial for self-employed professionals, as it can lead to repeat business, referrals and long-term success.

Momentum is essential for driving business growth in your self-employment venture. As you progress and achieve results, you gain the confidence and resources to invest in your business's expansion. You may have the opportunity to increase your rates or prices, hire additional help, invest in marketing or advertising, or diversify your offerings. Momentum allows you to take calculated risks and seize business opportunities that can help you grow and thrive as a self-employed professional.

WHAT

Building momentum in your business is the process of gaining positive and consistent progress towards your business goals. It involves taking intentional actions, creating strategies and maintaining a proactive mindset to keep your business moving forward and growing.

Clarity of focus is one of the most powerful tools in your arsenal when you are looking to build momentum for your business. Where do you see yourself or your business in one year? How about three years or even five years down the line? It may not be the most original question, but it's a great place to start. The clearer your goal, the easier it is to build momentum and chart a course towards it.

Let's say you are a freelance content creator specialising in sustainability topics. Your short-term goal could be to establish yourself as a go-to expert in the local sustainability scene, securing contracts with eco-conscious businesses. Your long-term vision might involve expanding your reach to a global audience, potentially through online courses or books. This clarity sharpens your focus and informs your day-to-day actions.

HOW

As a self-employed entrepreneur, you have the freedom to chart your own path and create your own destiny. Building momentum propels you to your goals by pushing you in the direction of your vision and mission. If you are not sure where to start, here are practical steps that will help you build the momentum you need to keep moving forward.

Define your vision and set clear goals

The first step in building momentum in your business is to define your vision and set clear goals. Your vision is the long-term direction and purpose of your business, while goals are the specific targets you want to achieve along the way.

When you have a clear vision and set measurable goals, you create a roadmap for your business, which provides you with a sense of direction and purpose. For example, if your vision is to become a leading consultant in your industry, your goals could be to acquire 10 new clients in the next six months, increase your revenue by 20% in the next year or launch a new online course within the next three months. This will help you stay focused and motivated, and as you make progress towards your goal, you will feel motivated and inspired to keep going.

Create a plan and take consistent action

Once you have defined your vision and set clear goals, the next step is to create a plan and take consistent action towards achieving those goals. Your plan should include the specific steps you will take to achieve your goals. To come up with a plan, start by breaking down your goals into smaller milestones with specific timelines. For example, if you want to double your revenue in a year, a monthly milestone could be to increase your revenue by 20% or acquire three new clients in a month. This sets you on a path towards your greater goal without overwhelming yourself. You can take gradual but consistent steps towards your goal in a way that is realistic and aligns with your other commitments and responsibilities.

Provide exceptional value to your clients

Providing exceptional value to your clients is a critical factor in building momentum in your business. Your clients are the lifeblood of your business, and satisfied clients are more likely to become repeat clients and refer your services to others. By exceeding your clients' expectations and delivering outstanding value, you can build a loyal client base that will support your business and help you gain momentum.

To provide exceptional value to your clients, focus on understanding their needs, wants and pain points. Listen to their feedback, communicate with them regularly and provide personalised solutions that address their specific challenges. Go the extra mile to deliver high-quality products or services that meet or exceed their expectations. Respond promptly to inquiries and be proactive in solving any issues that may arise. Cultivate a client-centric mindset and prioritise client satisfaction as a core value of your business. Happy clients are more likely to become loyal advocates who promote your business through word-of-mouth, testimonials and online reviews.

Build your network and collaborate

Building a strong network and collaborating with others can be a powerful way to build momentum in your business. Networking allows you to connect with like-minded individuals, potential clients and other entrepreneurs who can provide support, advice and opportunities for growth. Identify relevant networking opportunities such as industry events, conferences, online forums and social media groups. Attend these events, participate in discussions and engage with others to build relationships and expand your network.

Collaborating with others can also be a powerful way to leverage your skills and resources to achieve your goals faster. Look for opportunities to collaborate with other entrepreneurs or businesses that complement your services or products. For example, if you are a marketing consultant, you could collaborate with a web developer to offer a complete package to clients. Collaboration can help you reach new audiences, expand your offerings and create innovative solutions that can set you apart from the competition.

Embrace innovation and adaptability

The business landscape is constantly evolving, and as a self-employed entrepreneur, you need to be agile and willing to embrace change to stay relevant and competitive. Look for opportunities to innovate and differentiate yourself from the competition. Stay updated with your industry's latest trends, technologies and best practices. Be open to feedback from clients, peers and mentors, and use it to adjust your products, services or business model.

Be flexible and willing to pivot when necessary. If you encounter challenges or setbacks, don't get discouraged. Instead, view them as opportunities to learn, grow and adapt your strategies. Be proactive in identifying and addressing potential obstacles or changes in the market, and be willing to make bold decisions to keep your business moving forward.

Invest in your personal and professional growth

Your personal and professional development plays a significant role in building momentum in your business. Continuous learning and improvement are essential for staying ahead of the competition, expanding your skills and knowledge, and growing your business.

Invest in your personal and professional development by acquiring new skills, staying updated with industry trends and seeking opportunities for growth. Attend workshops, seminars, webinars or online courses related to your field to enhance your expertise. Read books, articles and blogs to stay informed about the latest developments in your industry.

Seek mentorship or coaching from experienced entrepreneurs or industry experts. Having a mentor or coach can provide you with valuable guidance, insights and accountability to help you overcome challenges and reach your business goals faster. Join industry associations or professional networks to connect with like-minded individuals and access resources, events and opportunities for professional growth.

Utilise social media and digital marketing

In today's digital age, social media and digital marketing are powerful tools for building momentum in your business. These platforms allow you to connect with your target audience, showcase your expertise and promote your products or services to a wider audience.

Develop a social media strategy that aligns with your business goals and target audience. Choose the right platforms where your ideal clients are active and create engaging and relevant content that resonates with them. Use social media to share valuable information, insights and updates about your business, and interact with your audience to build relationships and create a community around your brand.

Additionally, leverage the power of online advertising to reach a wider audience and promote your products or services. Platforms like Google Ads and social media advertising allow you to target specific demographics, interests and behaviours, making your marketing efforts more effective and efficient.

Track your progress and make data-driven decisions

To build momentum in your business, it's crucial to track your progress and make data-driven decisions. Monitoring and analysing your business performance can provide valuable insights into what's working and what's not, allowing you to make informed decisions to optimise your strategies and accelerate your momentum.

Set **key performance indicators** (KPIs) that align with your business goals and regularly track and measure your progress. Use analytics tools, such as Google Analytics or social media insights, to gather data and analyse your performance. Monitor your website traffic, engagement on social media, conversion rates, client feedback and other relevant metrics to assess the effectiveness of your strategies and identify areas for improvement.

For example, if you notice that a particular social media platform is driving more traffic to your website, consider allocating more resources to that platform. If you identify a drop in conversion rates on your website, analyse the possible reasons and make necessary changes to improve the user experience and increase conversions.

Stay persistent and resilient

Building momentum in your business is not always easy, and you may face challenges, setbacks and failures along the way. However, it's important to stay persistent and resilient in the face of adversity. Remember that success rarely comes overnight, and building a successful business takes time, effort and perseverance.

When facing challenges, view them as opportunities to learn and grow rather than roadblocks. Analyse the situation objectively, identify the root causes of the challenge and develop strategies to overcome it. Seek support from mentors, peers or a business coach who can provide guidance, encouragement and perspective.

Do not forget to celebrate your small wins and milestones along the way. Recognise and appreciate your progress, no matter how small it may seem. Celebrating your achievements will boost your motivation, morale and confidence and keep you motivated to continue pushing forward.

Take care of yourself

As a self-employed entrepreneur, it's easy to get caught up in the hustle and bustle of building your business, and neglecting your wellbeing can lead to burnout, which can hinder your momentum. It's crucial to take care of yourself physically, mentally and emotionally to ensure that you have the energy and resilience to keep pushing forward.

Make sure to get enough sleep, eat well and exercise regularly. Take breaks throughout your day to recharge and relax. Practice stress management techniques, such as meditation, mindfulness or yoga, to help you stay focused, calm and balanced.

Nurture your relationships with family and friends, and make time for hobbies and activities you enjoy. Taking care of yourself will not only benefit your wellbeing but also your business, as you will be better equipped to handle challenges, make sound decisions and maintain the motivation and drive needed to build momentum in your business.

WHAT IF

Failing to build momentum in your business as a self-employed entrepreneur can have several negative consequences. Here are some potential outcomes of failing to build momentum in your business:

Stagnation: Without momentum, your business may stagnate; meaning, it remains at the same level without significant growth or progress. This can result in a lack of excitement and motivation, leading to complacency and a loss of competitive advantage. Stagnation can also affect your revenue and profitability, as your business may struggle to attract new clients or retain existing ones.

Missed opportunities: Building momentum in your business opens opportunities for growth and expansion. Without momentum, you may miss out on opportunities to expand your client base, enter new markets, launch new products or services or establish strategic partnerships. This can result in missed revenue and growth potential and limit your business's ability to stay ahead of competitors.

Financial challenges: Building momentum in your business often requires investments in marketing, technology, talent and other resources. Without momentum, your business may struggle to generate sufficient revenue or cash flow to support these investments. This can result in financial challenges, such as cash flow issues, debt accumulation and inability to reinvest in your business for growth. It may also impact your personal finances; as a self-employed entrepreneur, your business's financial performance is closely linked to your personal income.

Loss of motivation and passion: Building momentum in your business involves setting and achieving goals, staying focused and overcoming challenges. When momentum is lacking, you may lose motivation and passion for your business. This can lead to a decline in your overall satisfaction and fulfilment as an entrepreneur, affecting your productivity, creativity and enthusiasm for your work. It may also impact your mental and emotional wellbeing, as the lack of progress and growth can cause stress, frustration and disappointment.

Decreased client engagement: Momentum in your business can positively impact client engagement and loyalty. When your business consistently makes progress and delivers value, it can attract and retain clients who are more likely to become loyal advocates and refer your business to others. However, without momentum, your business may struggle to maintain client engagement, resulting in decreased client loyalty and reduced repeat business.

Competitive disadvantage: In today's competitive business landscape, building momentum is crucial to stay ahead of the competition. Without momentum, your business may fall behind competitors actively building momentum through innovation, marketing, client engagement and other strategic initiatives. This can result in a competitive disadvantage, as your business may struggle to keep up with changing client preferences, market trends and technological advancements.

Loss of business sustainability: Building momentum is essential for the long-term sustainability of your business. Without momentum, your business may lack the resilience and agility needed to adapt to changing market dynamics and overcome obstacles. This can result in a loss of business sustainability, as your business may struggle to survive in a constantly evolving business environment.

3 ACTION QUESTIONS

1. What is your clear and compelling value proposition?

A clear and compelling value proposition is essential for building momentum in your business. It defines what makes your products or services unique and valuable to your target audience. Having a clear and compelling value proposition helps you differentiate yourself in the market, attract clients and build momentum in your business.

2. How will you consistently engage with your target audience?

Consistently engaging with your target audience is critical for building momentum in your business. It helps you establish relationships, create brand awareness and nurture client loyalty.

3. How will you continuously innovate and adapt to changing market dynamics?

Innovation and adaptability are key drivers of business momentum. As a self-employed entrepreneur, it's important to continuously innovate and adapt to changing market dynamics to stay relevant and competitive.

12.

Sustain yourself for the long term

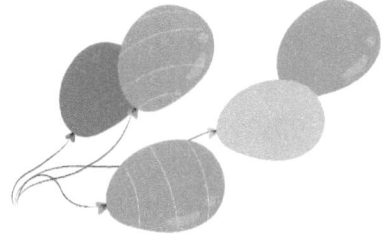

WHAT

Venturing into self-employment can be an exciting time in your professional journey. The prospect of having complete autonomy, financial reward and work-life balance can make all the challenges you will encounter on the way seem like a small price to pay. However, as fulfilling as charting your own course and following your passions are, it's important to remember that self-employment does not make you immune to burnout. In fact, in some cases, it may make you even more susceptible since you will rely solely on your energy, resources and expertise to keep everything together.

If you want to achieve sustainable success in your business, it is important to understand how to sustain yourself in business. As a new entrepreneur, getting your venture off the ground can be overwhelming, which could lead you to overlook important aspects such as your health, work-life balance and investing in new skills. It's crucial to recognise that your wellbeing and work-life balance play key roles in your long-term success. For example, if you are working long hours, which starts to impact your health, your productivity will suffer and affect the success of your business.

Achieving sustainable success in your business is a long-term endeavour that requires you to sustain yourself effectively. As a new entrepreneur, it's easy to become so engrossed in building your business that you overlook your health, work-life balance and skill development. However, these elements are not just peripheral concerns but the foundation upon which your business's long-term sustainability rests.

Your health is your most valuable asset, and it directly impacts your ability to run your business effectively. Ignoring your wellbeing can lead to burnout, stress-related health issues and decreased productivity. Remember that a healthy entrepreneur is more resilient, better equipped to handle challenges and has the stamina for the marathon that is self-employment. If you are constantly stressed out and emotionally and mentally drained, it will be hard to keep up with the demands of a new and growing business.

Work-life balance is a fundamental aspect of a successful and fulfilling life, especially when navigating the challenges and opportunities of self-employment. This balance involves effectively juggling the demands of your work with your personal life to ensure that neither suffers at the expense of the other. Self-employment often involves long hours, high stress and a relentless pursuit of business goals. This often makes new entrepreneurs likely to neglect the need for rest and personal time, resulting in burnout. This will not only impact your physical and mental health but can also harm your business by diminishing your creativity and productivity.

The essence of a balanced life is enjoying a good quality of life while doing the things you need to do professionally to advance your career, business and financial goals. Striking this delicate balance allows you to allocate time to activities that bring you joy, whether it's spending time with family, pursuing hobbies or simply relaxing. This will ensure that other aspects of your life, like personal relationships, self-care and self-improvement, are not neglected.

A fulfilling personal life will enhance your overall wellbeing and keep you motivated and energetic, positively impacting your business. Balanced individuals tend to have healthier relationships. Neglecting your personal life in favour of work can strain relationships with your family and friends, which is detrimental since you will need a strong support system for emotional and practical support during the ups and downs of entrepreneurship.

Paradoxically, taking time for yourself and balancing work and life can lead to increased productivity. When you have designated work hours and personal time, you're more likely to efficiently use your work hours and focus on what truly matters.

Apart from your personal wellbeing, continuous self-improvement is also crucial if you want to sustain yourself in business. Industries and markets are constantly changing, and as a self-employed professional, you will need to keep up with these changes to remain relevant. This means attending relevant seminars and classes or even going back to school if you feel that you need to boost your credentials or acquire new skills.

Investing in yourself is necessary in your journey as a self-employed professional because it allows you to stay competitive and maintain your UVP. For instance, if you're a midlife professional in the IT sector, staying current with programming languages or cybersecurity trends will allow you to pivot with market demands.

WHY

When you venture into self-employment, it's important to take a long-term view. This means considering what you need to do both on a personal and professional level to sustain yourself in business long-term.

When considering how to plan for the future, start by evaluating the kind of outcomes you want in your business and personal life. This means that while charting your revenue objectives, don't overlook plans for self-improvement, nurturing personal relationships and maintaining your health. Adopting this holistic approach throughout your self-employment journey helps you harmonise various facets of your life, fostering a healthy balance.

While making money is great, the beauty of self-employment is that it gives you agency to create a sustainable and fulfilling life that encompasses both your professional and personal aspirations. This balanced perspective ensures that your self-employment journey is not only financially rewarding but also emotionally and mentally enriching.

HOW

The initial stages of a self-employment venture can be exhilarating as you see your business gaining momentum and attracting clients. However, amid the excitement, it's crucial to maintain a long-term perspective and prioritise sustainability. Many entrepreneurs, especially those in service-based professions, tend to work tirelessly to meet client demands and grow their businesses. While dedication is admirable, it can lead to burnout if not balanced with sustainable practices.

If you are not sure how to navigate the complexities of self-employment while maintaining a healthy work-life balance, these strategies will guide you in sustaining yourself in business long term.

Time management

Time management is a critical skill for midlife professionals venturing into self-employment. It allows you to make the most of your work hours, maintain a healthy work-life balance and ensure your business remains sustainable. Fortunately, the time management skills that you learned as an employed professional will also serve you well in your own business.

The first and most basic step in time management is maintaining a daily schedule. A daily schedule that outlines your work hours, including breaks, will give structure to your day and allow you to maintain consistency in your life.

Start each day by identifying your most important tasks. Focus on completing these tasks first, as they have the greatest impact on your business's success. Allocate specific time blocks for different types of tasks. For instance, set aside dedicated blocks for client work, administrative tasks and personal development. Doing this ensures that you are not spending significant blocks of time on tasks that can be delegated or handled once or twice a week. For example, you do not want to allocate the most productive hours of your day to respond to emails; sectioning blocks of time for such tasks ensures that they do not impact your productivity or take up more time than necessary.

When you are just getting started in self-employment, it is normal to want to do everything yourself. However, one of the most important skills in time management is knowing when to outsource or delegate. Identify tasks that can be delegated or outsourced to free up your time for higher-value activities. For example, hiring a virtual assistant to handle administrative tasks will free up your time for more important tasks.

Getting familiar with productivity tools and apps is also an effective way to learn time management. Calendar apps can help you keep track of your schedule, including important meetings or even things in your personal life that need to be prioritised. You can also invest in project management software and note-taking apps to help you stay organised.

One of the most challenging issues newly self-employed professionals struggle with is knowing when to say **no**. It can be difficult setting boundaries, especially when you first start attracting clients to your business. This can cause you to overextend yourself or take on projects that may not be beneficial for your business. Knowing when to say no can help you avoid taking on more than you can handle and choose what projects to engage in. Remember that sustainable business success isn't just about initial growth; it's about building a business that thrives for years to come.

Education

Education is one of my top passions. As a secondary school teacher for 20 years and an adult tutor/trainer for more than 10 years, I have had the pleasure and privilege of having many groups of learners as part of classes, workshops and seminars.

People often look at my qualifications and think I must have been born on some other planet; why would I want to learn that much stuff? My reply is always "It is not about the bits of paper or the number of books I have read or how many assignments I have had to complete. Instead, what it was and is about is the journey on the way – the people I have met, the opportunities that have opened to me, the expansion and stretching of my own thinking, thoughts and ideas."

Education as a businesswoman is important. It does not necessarily mean traditional certificates, diplomas and degrees, but what it does mean is to have a burning desire as well as the means to make sure that learning never ends. Education must be lifelong. It is about growing your skills, your character and your knowledge just a little bit each day.

Don't Just Dream It, Do It!

I read a great article in the Huffington Post, titled What Does It Mean to Be Well-Educated? by Sabrina Stevens. Sabrina defines an educated person as someone who has the habits of mind, hand and heart to adapt to whatever life might throw at them. Wow, I love that definition! Life does have its curve balls; how do you handle them? How are your flexibility skills? Can you bend and shape yourself for new circumstances and new surroundings?

What about the skill sets you need as a business owner? There are so much quality content available on the internet that can increase your expertise and knowledge as a business owner. There are lots of online courses available; many of them are free, or at least at reasonable prices. I love the website www.udemy.com, which has an incredible array of courses to choose from in several areas. Start with a course just to blow a few cobwebs out if you haven't committed yourself to doing much new learning lately.

Don't view education through the lens of your primary and secondary school days – many, unfortunately, don't have great memories of those days (except, of course, if you happen to have been in my class!). Instead, I want to encourage you to view education as a toolbox of learnings that you carry about and add to day by day. Not only do you carry that toolbox about, but you use and apply the tools.

Self-employment is an opportunity for continuous professional development. Set milestones for enhancing your expertise and expanding your knowledge base. This can involve attending industry conferences, pursuing certifications or exploring new niches within your field.

Sustain yourself for the long term

In today's fast-paced business landscape, industries are constantly evolving, and new technologies emerge regularly. To remain competitive and provide value to your clients, you must stay updated with the latest trends, tools and best practices. Acquiring new skills allows you to diversify your offerings and cater to a broader range of client needs.

Health and wellness

Health goals have always been the biggest challenge for me – I can set and achieve a lot of other types of goals in my life, but the health-focused ones seem to elude me at the best of times. As a teenager I had anorexia; I was the best at hiding food, throwing up food and avoiding food altogether. It took me to my mid-20s to get myself into more balanced and healthy eating patterns. In my 20s, when my body was more flexible, I managed to run, swim and bike quite regularly and enjoyed some games of tennis.

As I got into my 30s and then 40s, I let my health slide, too busy caring for others and their health and not being mindful of my own. I was diagnosed with fibromyalgia, which really knocked me around pain-wise; I certainly learned to cope with new pain thresholds, and some days just a walk to the letterbox is all I could muster. In my late 30s my body went through some more trauma, as I had two miscarriages and an ectopic pregnancy – pain, chocolate, heartache, chocolate, grief and loss, chocolate, hormones and chocolate! Oh, and did I say chocolate?

Gals, I know we all have our own stories to tell when it comes to our health, and we deal with our aches and pains and hormones and emotions in a variety of ways. What I am sharing here is the reality of my health struggles, not because I want sympathy and choruses of "oh, poor you" but because I want to be real. I want to encourage you to find what works for you and your health – whether that's strolling in the countryside, working out at the gym or following a health program such as keeping yourself flexible through yoga.

Do what it takes for you – not someone else, but you – to gain a level of wellness and health that will enable you to live a sustainable, adventure-filled life; one that sustains you in business. Do just that small step: make yourself avocado and eggs on toast for brekkie tomorrow; the next day, dip your toes in the ocean and walk along the beach for 30 minutes; the next day, download a From-Couch-to-5K app on your phone and start with Day 1.

If you're tracking well with your health, encourage others – walk, run, swim alongside them or make some yummy, healthy meals they can put in their freezer. As women, we need to be healthy to retain and enhance our value – inside and out.

Take time off

Don't neglect taking holidays. Unplug from your business during vacations to recharge and prevent burnout. Taking time off is a crucial component of maintaining a healthy work–life balance and ensuring your sustainability as a self-employed professional. Continuous work without breaks can lead to burnout, which can have severe physical and mental health consequences. Regular holiday breaks provide an opportunity to recharge, reduce stress and prevent burnout. Telltale signs that you might need some time off to recharge include lack of focus, waning creativity and lack of motivation.

Vacation time doesn't have to be long to be effective. Sometimes even just a weekend away with your loved ones can be enough to re-energise you when you get back to business. Pay attention to your mental and physical health – your body usually gives you signs that you may be overdoing things and need to take a break. You may think that continuously putting in hours on end is the most productive approach, but stepping away from work from time to time allows your mind to rest and rejuvenate, leading to increased focus, creativity and efficiency.

Have you ever found yourself staring at a computer screen or the same page in a book and feeling like you're not absorbing anything? Mental exhaustion can make even the simplest tasks feel like an uphill battle. It's crucial to recognise these moments and allow yourself to take a step back when you feel overwhelmed. As a midlife professional, you are your business's most valuable asset, so taking care of yourself is an integral part of ensuring the long-term sustainability of your business.

WHAT IF

Sustaining yourself in business can be a delicate balancing act. It involves managing various aspects of your professional and personal life to ensure that you remain productive, healthy and fulfilled. If you do not take a holistic approach that considers business goals along with personal development and self-care, you may potentially face the following challenges.

> **Burnout:** Overworking and neglecting self-care can result in burnout. Burnout is characterised by physical and emotional exhaustion, reduced productivity and a sense of disillusionment. This can severely hinder your

ability to perform well in your business and negatively affect your mental and physical health.

Stagnation: Without continuous learning and skill development, you may stagnate in your profession. In rapidly evolving industries, staying static can lead to obsolescence, making it challenging to remain competitive or adapt to changing market demands.

Health issues: Ignoring your health and wellbeing can lead to various health problems, including stress-related illnesses, sleep disorders and lifestyle diseases. These health issues can reduce your overall quality of life and impact your ability to work effectively.

Financial instability: Without proper financial planning and a safety net, you may find it challenging to weather financial setbacks, such as a drop in income or unexpected expenses. This can lead to financial stress and instability, both personally and in your business.

Isolation: Failing to build a support network and neglecting personal relationships can lead to feelings of isolation and loneliness. This lack of social support can affect your emotional wellbeing and hinder your personal and professional growth.

Inefficiency: Poor time management and the absence of work-life boundaries can result in inefficient work habits. You may spend excessive time on tasks that don't yield significant results, hindering your business's growth and profitability.

Limited growth: Focusing solely on the day-to-day operations of your business without investing in personal development and building a network can hinder your business's potential for growth and expansion.

3 ACTION QUESTIONS

1. What are your main long-term goals and priorities, on a business and personal level?

Define your core values and priorities in your personal life and business. What truly matters to you? Is it spending quality time with family, pursuing personal interests or achieving specific business goals? Understanding your priorities will help you make decisions that align with your values.

2. Do you have clear boundaries between your work/business and personal life?

Establish clear boundaries between work and personal life. Determine when and where work should take place and when it's time to step away from work-related tasks. Define limits for working hours, responding to emails and taking breaks. Having well-defined boundaries is crucial for maintaining a healthy work-life balance.

3. How do you and how will you invest in yourself, long term?

Develop a plan for continuous self-improvement. Identify areas where you want to grow personally and professionally and create strategies to invest in your development. This may include setting aside time for learning, attending workshops or courses or seeking mentorship. Prioritising self-investment ensures that you remain competitive and adaptable in your field.

Appendix

5+U Pillars of Business Start-up and Development Model©

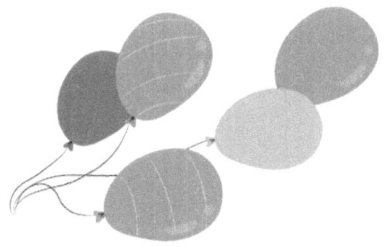

The 5+U Pillars of Business Start-up and Development Model© is a series of questions to help you identify the range of matters you need to consider both when starting out and as you develop your business. If you have already begun your business, you can use the set of questions to reflect on matters that you have not addressed and/or that you need to sharpen and make changes to.

Pillar 1: Strategic matters

1. What is your story or background or experience?
2. What are your skills?
3. What are your passions and interests?
4. What does an ideal work/business day look like for you?
5. What are the business ideas you have?
6. How will you generate income from your business ideas?
7. What income streams will you have?
8. What products can you create from your services?
9. What services can you create from your products?
10. What are the strengths, weaknesses, opportunities and threats of your business ideas?
11. What problem/s will your business solve?
12. What are your business goals – short-term, medium term, long-term?
13. Do you intend to build your business as a saleable asset? If so, how do you intend to do this over what timeframe?

Pillar 2: Legal compliance matters

Disclaimer: Please ensure you refer to the legal compliance matters relevant to your own country/state.

1. Have you registered for a Business Tax Number?
2. Have you registered your business name?
3. Have you registered your domain name (URL) for your website and email address?
4. What insurance will you need – for example, Public Liability, Public Indemnity, Vehicle, Inventory?
5. What licenses and/or legal permissions do you need – a food handling license, for example?

6. What associations or memberships do you need to belong to and/or would you benefit from?
7. What certificates or training do you need for the products/services your business will provide?
8. What employment contracts, service agreements and/or other legal documentation (for example, a trademark for your logo, a lease for office premises) do you need?
9. What will be the legal structure for your business?

Pillar 3: Marketing matters

1. Have you conducted market research – that is, is there a demand for your product/service?
2. Who will be your clients?
3. Who will be your ideal client?
4. How much are your clients willing to pay?
5. Who is your competition?
6. Will you have a pilot phase for the business to test the market?
7. What will be your business name, logo, tagline and branding colours?
8. What social media platforms are you going to use?
9. What range of marketing collateral will you have – for example, flyers, brochures, business cards, car magnets, fridge magnets, promotional products (keyring, USB, hat, pen), banner?
10. Will you create a business capability statement and/or portfolio to showcase your business?
11. What will be your four to five marketing actions each week?
12. What type of website (for example, ecommerce to sell products) do you want?

Pillar 4: Operational matters, including human resources and IT

1. Where will you run your business from?
2. What equipment and/or stock do you need for your business?
3. What are the risks associated with running your business?
4. What staff will you need for the business?
5. What will be your operating procedures?
6. What will be your recruitment and induction processes?
7. Have you created an email account for the business?
8. What computer or IT equipment do you need?
9. How will you take electronic payments?
10. What apps will you use in your business to increase efficiency?
11. What voice message and email signature will you have?

Pillar 5: Financial matters

1. Have you opened a separate bank account for your business?
2. What will be your recordkeeping processes?
3. What accounting software will you use?
4. Have you found a bookkeeper/accountant to help guide your business's financial matters?
5. What financial documents do you need – for example, receipts, quotes, invoices, etc?
6. What will be your terms and conditions of payment, charging of deposits and terms of credit?
7. Are you aware of your tax obligations?
8. What will be your policies for financial processes – for example, Debt Collection Policy?

9. What are your projected expenses and sales for the business?
10. What wage or salary will you pay yourself from the business?

Pillar U (You): You, the business owner

1. Who will you have as the "Cheering Squad" for your business?
2. What coaching/mentoring will you participate in?
3. What networking opportunities align with your business?
4. What computer skills do you have, and what computer skills do you need to learn?
5. What professional development or skill-building do you need to do?
6. What will self-care as a business owner look like for you?
7. How many weeks in a year do you intend to run your business?
8. What breaks do you plan to take, and how will you ensure the business still runs well during those break times?
9. Which personal areas in your life that may impact you as a business owner do you need to get professional support on navigating – for example, anxiety in networking situations?

Other books by Maree Cutler-Naroba

Maree is the author of ARISE: Awakening Christian Women Entrepreneurs to Shift the Course of History (July 2023).

> Deborah of the bible was an incredible woman of God; she was a Kingdom Pioneer who boldly took hold of her God-given gifts and talents and stepped out in faith. She knew that in her God anything was possible. This book is a clarion call for modern-day Mighty Deborah Christian Women Entrepreneurs to take action and pioneer globally, with prophetic purpose, planning and prayer, the business ventures God has placed in their hearts.
>
> **Order from: https://www.amazon.com/ARISE-Awakening-Christian-Entrepreneurs-History/dp/0645782718**

About the author

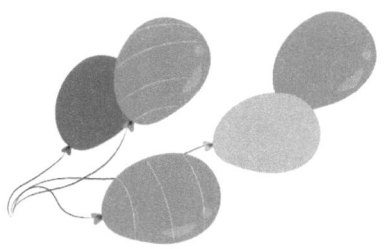

Maree Cutler-Naroba currently resides in regional North West Australia with her husband, Tevita Naroba. She is pursuing a PhD exploring the potential of small business as a therapeutic trauma recovery tool for women with a lived experience of complex trauma, turning pain into purpose.

Maree Cutler-Naroba –
linkedin.com/in/maree-cutler-naroba

Maree is a multi-passionate woman who loves to serve people through the gifts and talents God has placed in her hands, as a prophetic pioneer for His Kingdom. Maree outworks the call of God on her life through a plethora of business and ministry ventures.

Through her business, **MCN Consulting**, Maree offers a variety of business strategic planning and entrepreneur education services to assist businesses in positioning themselves for impact and legacy. One of the specialities of MCN Consulting is supporting women living in remote, rural or regional areas. Additionally, as a multidisciplinary, trauma-informed practitioner, Maree focuses on working with clients, communities and organisations for whom the application of a trauma-informed lens is central to their growth and development.

www.mcn-consulting.com

MCN Consulting has four sister businesses, **Mind that Gap Studio** (content and course creation for service professionals), **Swirl** (online business coaching and design services for midlife professional women), **MCN Dream Nurturer** (supporting women to turn their adversity into service) and **Boomers Biz Gym** (entrepreneur education and coaching for new business owners 50+).

www.mcn-consulting.com.au/mind-that-gap-studio
www.justswirl.com.au
www.mareecutlernaroba.com
www.facebook.com/boomersinbizforacause

Maree founded **The Deborah Conference** as a tool to inspire Christian women entrepreneurs to live a business life of passionate pursuit and purpose wrapped in His presence. This conference sits within the **Deborah Business Education Hub** (DBEH), which focuses on Christ-centred business education. The DBEH provides support, inspiration, impartation and prayer to champion the faith-filled business journey of Christian women entrepreneurs and includes **Deborah Women in Business Collective** chapters, which assist in developing microbusiness ventures of rural women in developing nations.

www.thedeborahconference.com
www.deborohbizedhub.com
www.deborahbizedhub.com/dwib-collective

The **Women Echo Him Collective** (WEHC), founded by Maree, is a global community of women who put the "trumpet" to their lips, praying and declaring God's heartbeat over towns, cities and nations.

www.wehcollective.com

The **Barnabas Legacy Children's Dream Foundation** (BLCDF) is a legally registered Ugandan Not for Profit Organisation in Jinja, Uganda. Maree is a Director and Board Chair of BLCDF and co-founder of the **Agape Star Christian School** (ASCS), which sits under the Foundation. The ASCS opened in February 2023 in Namatovu Village, Jinja, Uganda. It is a school that caters for over 250 primary and secondary school students.

www.barnabaslegacy.org
www.barnabaslegacy.org/agape-star-christian-school

www.ingramcontent.com/pod-product-compliance
Lightning Source LLC
Chambersburg PA
CBHW020139130526
44591CB00030B/140